A Challenge To Change

The Language
Learning Continuum

A Challenge To Change

The Language Learning Continuum

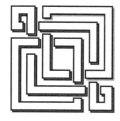

Strategies for More Effective Language Instruction

Lessons Learned From the Articulation and
Achievement Project

Claire W. Jackson, Executive Editor

College Entrance Examination Board
New York

Founded in 1900, the College Board is a not-for-profit educational association that supports academic preparation and transition to higher education for students around the world through the ongoing collaboration of its member schools, colleges, universities, educational systems and organizations.

In all of its activities, the Board promotes equity through universal access to high standards of teaching and learning and sufficient financial resources so that every student has the opportunity to succeed in college and work.

The College Board champions—by means of superior research; curricular development; assessment; guidance, placement, and admission information; professional development; forums; policy analysis; and public outreach—educational excellence for all students.

Editorial inquiries should be addressed to Publications Services, The College Board, 45 Columbus Avenue, New York, NY 10023-6992.

Copies of this book may be ordered from College Board Publications, Box 886, New York, NY 10101-0886, (800) 323-7155, or online at www.collegeboard.org. The price is $13.00.

Credits for artwork:
p. 76, *July 28, 1830: Liberty Guiding the People*, Eugene Delacroix (1798–1863), Louvre, ©Photo RMN, H. Lewandowski.

p. 77, *The Representatives of Foreign Powers Coming to Salute the Republic as a Sign of Peace*, Henri Rousseau (1844–1910), Paris, Musée Picasso, ©Photo RMN, R.G. Ojeda.

Library of Congress Catalog Card Number: 98-074400
International Standard Book Number: 0-87447-606-2

Printed in the United States of America.

PRINCIPAL WRITERS AND CONSULTANTS

Claire W. Jackson
Assistant Superintendent for Curriculum and Instruction
Brookline Public Schools
Brookline, Massachusetts

Donald H. Reutershan, Jr.
Regional Education Service Representative
Specialty Area, Modern and Classical Languages
Maine Department of Education
Augusta, Maine

Elizabeth Alexander
Curriculum and Assessment Coordinator
Burlington High School
Burlington, Vermont

Janice Darias
World Language Coordinator
Belmont Public Schools
Belmont, Massachusetts

Robert Fournier
Foreign Language Consultant
Suncook, New Hampshire

Mary Ann M. Hansen
State World Languages Consultant
Connecticut Department of Education
Hartford, Connecticut

Jessica H. Noyes
Teacher of Spanish
U-32 High School
Montpelier, Vermont

June K. Phillips
Dean of Arts and Sciences
Weber State University
Ogden, Utah

Harry L. Rosser
Associate Professor of Spanish
Department of Romance Languages and Literatures
Boston College
Chestnut Hill, Massachusetts

Contents

Articulation and Achievement: From Theory to Practice

The publication in 1996 of *Articulation and Achievement: Connecting Standards, Performance, and Assessment in Foreign Language* (Jackson, et al., 1996) marked the end of the first stage of a significant teacher-based effort aimed at developing textbook-free, articulated standards for student performance supported and validated by matching assessments. Funded by the United States Department of Education's Fund for the Improvement of Postsecondary Education (FIPSE) and supported by the College Board and the American Council on the Teaching of Foreign Languages (ACTFL), the Articulation and Achievement project brought together a group of outstanding language teachers from demographically diverse secondary and postsecondary institutions across the six New England states under the leadership of Claire Jackson, Foreign Languages department chair at Newton South High School in Massachusetts, and Donald Reutershan, foreign language consultant for the Maine Department of Education. They were assisted by June Phillips, dean of Arts and Humanities at Weber State University and director of the National Standards in Foreign Language Education project; Nancy Anderson, a senior examiner at the Educational Testing Service and a specialist in language teaching and learning; and Harry Rosser, professor of Spanish literature at Boston College and author of several highly respected language textbooks. This group, together with more than 20 classroom teachers, worked together over the course of three years in an effort to uncover more effective ways to achieve higher levels of student learning.

The principal goals of this project were to study actual classroom practice in grades 7-14 in a variety of rural, urban, and suburban sites in order to acquire a deeper understanding of individual student progress, to develop classroom-based assessments to confirm that understanding, and to improve instruction. The participants also sought to find practical ways to extend student learning by addressing the critical issue of the relationship between well-articulated programs and achievement, particularly at the critical transition points between middle and high school and high school and college.

During the course of the project, participants assessed the performance of nearly 3,000 students in grades 7-14 using oral and written prompts. (See Appendix B.) What they discovered over the three-year span of the project deeply changed the way these teachers viewed student progress. Many of their initial assumptions about what students know were proven wrong. More important, they found their assumptions about what their students could do to be vastly overstated. They realized that the distance between their instructional goals and the actual outcomes they were achieving was far greater than anticipated. These revelations resulted in a collective decision to document actual student performance, to gather diverse samples of student work at each stage of language learning to confirm their findings, and to provide a concrete basis for final revisions to their work. Students' work samples were collected and evaluated throughout the course of the project, and templates were designed for student portfolios. (See Appendix D.) Throughout the three-year period, participants enlisted the assistance of colleagues in reviewing and refining performance descriptions.

The immediate outcomes of this work were:

1. The development of the Language Learning Continuum, which fully defines and describes the measurable characteristics of each of five stages in student linguistic development between middle school and the sophomore year in college. (See Chapter 2.)

2. The creation of a variety of effective and practical classroom-based performance assessments including a new format for summative assessment called "integrated assessment." (See Appendix C.)

3. The collection of large numbers of student samples that were used to validate the Language Learning Continuum as it developed and that have proven enormously helpful in

the follow-up seminars and workshops with teachers at national and regional conferences. It is estimated that in the past four years, over 5,000 teachers have either participated in these workshops, or read the Articulation and Achievement report, or both. Project participants report that the message they bring to colleagues has been easily understood and enthusiastically received; they also report that teachers have asked for more information about the Language Learning Continuum, more samples of student work, and more examples of good assessment strategies for the classroom.

This book is a serious effort to respond to those requests and to suggest ways in which the language teaching profession can profit from the lessons project participants learned by increased understanding of the performance factors that need to drive instruction—the very factors that cause some students to succeed while many others fail and give up the study of languages entirely.

The Articulation and Achievement Project was conceived and carried out between 1991 and 1997. The classroom teachers who participated in the project began by using an instructional model that evolved from the 1986 ACTFL *Proficiency Guidelines*. At a time when K-12 programs remain the exception rather than the rule in most school districts in New England and elsewhere, this work represents and reflects the practical realities of teaching and learning. While we continually aspire to and work toward the goals of the *Standards for Foreign Language Learning*, this book does not attempt to show how the *Standards* themselves have influenced and changed instruction. Both projects serve to reinforce and enhance one another.

This book aims to help classroom teachers be more effective and places particular emphasis on the importance of better articulation based on fuller understanding of student performance. Those of us who participated in this project hope that *A Challenge to Change* will provide support and guidance for improved instruction as we move toward realizing the goals of the *Standards for Foreign Language Learning*.

REFERENCES

Jackson, Claire, et al. 1996. *Articulation and Achievement: Connecting Standards, Performance, and Assessment in Language*. New York: College Entrance Examination Board.

CHAPTER 1

GREAT EXPECTATIONS: STANDARDS, PERFORMANCE, AND ACCOUNTABILITY

I f a single word could be chosen to characterize the current focus in education resulting from the reform efforts of the 1990s, that word would have to be "performance." While the development of learning standards at the national, state, and local levels provided answers to the critical query, "What *should* all students know and be able to do?", the central question that has now evolved is "What *do* all students know and what are they able to do?" The focus has changed from content to performance, and hence, to assessment. Embedded in this question is another equally compelling and complex issue—accountability. Individual teachers, schools, school districts, and states are trying to establish systems that respond to the public demand for accountability. The nation as a whole is involved in a highly debated examination of education's "value-added" factor, that is, the measurable gains in students' learning as determined by both performance and achievement. What is being sought is a clearer understanding of the connection between what is taught and what is actually learned and data upon which to base plans for improving curriculum, instruction, and learning nationwide.

Given this result-oriented environment, it is not surprising to find researchers and practitioners working together to find new ways to measure student progress in valid and reliable contexts that support instruction and that will enrich and expand upon traditional standardized testing as the single most important, universally understood measure of student learning. The College Board has long been interested in the measurement of student performance; the Advanced Placement Examination (AP®) is one of the most highly respected examples of a hybrid test that measures both what students know and what they are able to do. Well-known experts in assessment, Grant Wiggins, Lauren Resnick, and Dennie Palmer Wolf, to name but a few, have devoted their professional lives to this topic, looking at performance-based assessment from all angles, from its practical class-room-based aspects to the more theoretical question of psychometric soundness.

While the implications of these developments are complex, one thing is clear: the movement toward more performance-based assessment, while not the sole solution, holds great promise for the foreign language profession because it enables teachers to plan assessment activities that are closely related to both short- and long-term goals and to develop good models that will inevitably lead to better instruction, improved professional development, and higher motivation on the part of learners. Finally, it will also inevitably lead to greater accountability resulting in the clarification of professional goals and providing the leverage necessary to correct current public misconceptions about the quality of the product we, as a profession, can deliver and the resources required to deliver it.

In "Curriculum and Assessment Standards: Common Measures or Conversations?", a chapter written for the 1994 College Board publication entitled *The Future of Education: Perspectives on National Standards in America*, Dennie Palmer Wolf discusses the role of national standards in the education landscape. She points out the current strong fiscal support provided to states that are developing improvement plans based on standards, and goes on to describe the reform process as a three-pronged wager.

> First, there is the bet that if minimum competency standards and standardized testing could drive the curriculum down to rote learning, then the inverse is possible. If we can formulate demanding national standards and equally demanding performance assessments, we can drive achievement up. The second bet is that, armed with national standards, we can achieve what years of desegregation have not yielded, equitable access to worthwhile educational activities like writing, problem-solving, and scientific experimentation. And finally, there is the bet that crisply formulated content and performance standards will (stimulate)…widespread agreement and equally clear implications. (p. 87)

The foreign language profession took the first significant steps toward meeting Wolf's challenge when the *Standards for Foreign Language Learning: Preparing for the 21st Century* were published by the American Council on the Teaching of Foreign Languages in 1996, with funding from the United States Department of Education. These standards, like those for other major disciplines that have appeared since the early 1990s, describe and define what all students in American schools should know, understand, and be able to do as a result of language instruction. (See Appendix A.)

STANDARDS FOR FOREIGN LANGUAGE LEARNING

The *Standards for Foreign Language Learning: Preparing for the 21st Century* represent the collective knowledge and wisdom of the entire language profession, addressing forcefully the issues Wolf raises in her discussion of performance standards for all students. The *Standards* challenge the American public to understand the critical importance of language learning. In clear and well-reasoned language, the *Standards* challenge local districts, states, and the national government to encourage and support, from the earliest age possible, the study of languages other than English. They also address the foreign language profession as a whole and challenge us to establish programs that create language learners; students who can communicate in and understand languages other than English using both the spoken and the written word; students who truly understand the importance and meaning of culture; students who use their knowledge of language to acquire knowledge of and insight into other disciplines; students whose understanding of their first language and culture is enhanced by their knowledge of another; and students who are ultimately able to use their knowledge of language beyond the school setting for enjoyment and enrichment. Thus, the *Standards* have both a political and a programmatic agenda.

Clearly, without the means to establish programs based on a continuum that begins early and extends throughout a child's educational career, we cannot meet the programmatic goals the *Standards* define. Before students can attain the complex linguistic goals of exchanging, supporting, and discussing opinions (*Standards*, p. 39), identifying and analyzing intangible products of the target culture such as political institutions (*Standards*, p. 48), comparing nuances of meanings of words (*Standards*, p. 57), discussing topics from other school subjects in the target language (*Standards*, p. 51), and consulting various sources in the language to obtain information, they need the time to acquire the language and to internalize what they have learned.

Many American teachers still believe that their most advanced language learners, after only six years of instruction, are able to perform at the level suggested by the *Standards* for grade 12. What we now understand is that under normal classroom conditions, it will actually take many more years of study than are currently available to most students in the United States to know and be able to do what the *Standards* describe. Yes, there may be some very gifted students who demonstrate extraordinary skill; others may have language experiences from home or from travel that accelerate their progress. Nevertheless, for most students, reaching these goals will require the amount of exposure and instruction suggested by the *Standards*—early and long. If this is really the case, then what are realistic goals for students who do not have the advantage of extended sequence? How can we best evaluate and improve student performance as we move toward longer sequences of study over the next decade?

The K-12 Student Standards Task Force, whose members developed the *Standards for Foreign Language Learning*, explored these issues, and the standards document emphasizes the importance of time in developing communicative competence. In addition, rather than focusing on the discrete skills of speaking, listening, reading, and writing, the Task Force highlighted the *purposes* of communication, thus broadening traditional concepts of language instruction. The *Standards* provide a rich context for creating extended-sequence programs that truly prepare students to communicate in languages other than English.

The *Standards* are broad and include a clear, unified blueprint for the future of language education. They lay the groundwork for developing state frameworks, local curricula, and specific classroom practices. The translation of the *Standards* into strategies for teaching and learning will prove to be rewarding if undertaken in the same spirit of expansive and creative thinking the *Standards* themselves reflect. Implementing the *Standards* will require close collaboration between and among members of the teaching community. Teachers of classical and modern languages; teachers at elementary, secondary, and post-secondary institutions; and teachers of language and literature will have to work together to establish articulated guidelines that will inform practice across the nation. Accomplishing this goal will take the kind of collective will and energy that result-ed in the development of the *Standards* themselves. Without such an effort, however, the expectation that the *Standards* will result in major and significant change is likely to remain an unfulfilled dream.

A CHALLENGE TO CHANGE

In spite of recent progress in the implementation of proficiency-based models, much of the foreign language curriculum and instruction across the nation is still based on a neat division of topics tied to increasingly difficult grammatical structures. Although learning a language is a complex, multifaceted experi-ence strongly influenced by many factors both inside and outside the classroom, formal language instruction and assessment are typically linear, involve learning the structure of the language, and are still measured by years of instruction completed rather than by the demonstrated competence of the learner. Perhaps the greatest contribution of the Standards Project will be a defin-itive shift away from this model. With the implicit understand-ing that learning a language is a lifelong experience and the explicit demand that this learning begin in kindergarten and extend through grade 12, the *Standards* validate and strengthen nationwide efforts to integrate foreign language instruction into the curriculum of the early grades.

By describing how a language is learned in terms of its purpose as a mode of communication, the *Standards* provide consistent operational guidelines for instruction that is content-based, encourages interdisciplinary learning, and meets the needs of all students. It is possible that the single greatest challenge the foreign language teaching profession will face in the years ahead is not the development of longer instructional sequences or the design of an integrated curriculum, but meeting the needs of *all* students. The question is not whether all students can learn a second language, but rather how programs can be designed that respect the varying rates at which students with differing abilities and language experience learn, while still challenging every student by maintaining high standards and offering stimulating subject matter.

Longer instructional sequences will promote developmental growth and support the creation of integrated models of instruction. As this evolves, teachers of foreign language will need to develop new skills and learn to apply new instructional strategies. They will need a more extensive background in the literature, art, and history of the people whose language they teach; they will need to rethink many of their beliefs about individual learning styles and become more knowledgeable about language acquisition. As foreign language educators define a coherent and consistent set of professional standards, postsecondary institutions must respond by preparing classroom teachers who meet those standards and who can successfully teach language in an increasingly complex environment.

The challenges posed by curriculum, instruction, and new assessment strategies must be addressed in the larger context of articulation. In the less-than-ideal model that constitutes common practice in the United States today, students move from level to level of foreign language study in a linear fashion. The levels may be described in terms of proficiency, but promotion through the system is too often determined by completion of a certain number of chapters in a textbook, or by demonstrated competence on a written examination. Although such tests may also include oral components, the ability to carry on a coherent conversation or to understand the authentic spoken language is rarely a determining factor in the decision to allow students to progress to the next level. The principal criterion remains overall passing grades, based primarily on written evidence of competence at a particular level of study. This familiar model fails to recognize the essential nature of language as communication, reinforces the traditional view of language study as the study of grammatical structure, and makes students feel less competent as they reach higher levels. The oral/aural components of instruction give way to increasing demands for grammatical competence. This model has, over the years, created a funnel through which it becomes increasingly difficult to pass. The resulting decline in grades as students progress, combined with the sometimes overwhelming demands to memorize grammatical structures and unrelated vocabulary, has resulted in an attrition rate that would be unacceptable in any other subject.

The challenge to the profession nationwide is to realize the promise of the *Standards for Foreign Language Learning*. Researchers and practitioners must continue the important work of developing content-based, culturally sensitive curricula. Postsecondary institutions will need to improve and expand current training programs for foreign language teachers. These efforts will require massive support at state and local levels in terms of planning time, flexible scheduling, adequate staffing, and financial and material resources. The teaching profession must address the issues of meeting the needs of all students, easing transitions from level to level and school to school, and, most important, creating a common language to describe student progress along a commonly understood language acquisition continuum.

THE HEART OF THE MATTER

If, as the *Standards for Foreign Language Learning* state, "Communication is at the heart of human experience," and if the ability to communicate in at least one language other than English is the fundamental goal of language instruction, then, as a profession, we have much to do before realizing that goal. The publication of the ACTFL *Proficiency Guidelines* in 1986 and the *Standards for Foreign Language Learning* in 1996 represent the first critical steps toward creating consensus about the importance of language learning, the nature of that learning, and what is needed to achieve proficiency or communicative competence. Nevertheless, in spite of the fact that there has been widespread professional support and acceptance of the concepts on which these documents are based, (i.e., long sequences that begin early in a child's career and consistent high-quality proficiency-based instruction) the promise of proficiency in a language other than English remains largely unfulfilled. The reasons are complex and have been discussed at length in every professional forum. On the practical level, in American classrooms, the obstacles are often overwhelming; relatively few programs begin before middle school, and class size is often too large to be effective. In addition, long-standing traditions such as college requirements that are translated into high school graduation requirements do little to encourage students to "start early and stay long."

Recognizing that the responsibility for achieving the promise was both a political and a professional one, the participants in the Articulation and Achievement Project set out, in their own local schools and colleges, to find more effective strategies for instruction that would yield increased student performance <u>within the constraints imposed by current educational practice</u>.

Clearly, the most compelling lesson participants learned from the Articulation and Achievement Project was the enormous significance of the counterproductive nature of the practice of defining student progress by years of study. Typically, second language courses are described and defined by the school year, i.e., Level I generally refers to the first school year of study at the high school level. While there are variations on this theme, middle schools often call the two or three years devoted to language study Level I, with the expectation that students leaving middle school will take Level II in high school. In cases where this is not true and each year is given a different number classification such as "Grade 7-French I" and "Grade 8-French II," teachers almost always understand and apply the goals of Level I language to these two years of study, often splitting a textbook between the years or actually purchasing the textbook in two parts, an accommodation made by publishers to meet the needs of younger middle school students. In the same mode, postsecondary institutions typically consider two years of high school study at the secondary level the equivalent of one year at the postsecondary level. In most cases, the course of study, as well as student achievement, is determined by the topics contained in the textbook chosen for use in the classroom. Consequently, the most critical component in articulation is often the textbook; students progress from the Level I text to the Level II text, and so on.

When one takes a moment to reflect on how language programs are articulated, level to level, based on "coverage" and expectations set by a diverse set of textbook publishers, it is easy to see why articulation is a nearly impossible goal and why so many students flounder, feel unrewarded for their efforts, and, ultimately discouraged, give up learning a second language in favor of other subjects. Sadly, this often happens after grade 10, at exactly the point when the years already invested in study would begin to pay off.

Participants in the Articulation and Achievement Project developed the Language Learning Continuum (printed in its entirety at the end of this chapter) in an effort to alter the focus of instruction and to move the profession toward a more flexible, practical approach to student achievement that sets high standards, is performance-based, and creates a "transition" language for identifying the major performance characteristics of each stage of language learning. With the assistance of good texts and thoughtful instruction, it can be used in any school system, college, or university to help students progress confidently and continue their study successfully through the advanced stages.

The Language Learning Continuum is a descriptive model of the way in which most English-speaking students actually perform as they progress through various levels of instruction in typical school settings. It is different from all other frameworks currently used to describe student performance in that each draft was revised over the course of the Articulation and Achievement Project to reflect the findings of the participants in their analyses of *actual* student performance as documented by classroom-based assessments. The performance levels described are the result of testing nearly 3,000 students in a wide variety of middle school, high school, and postsecondary settings. In this way, the performance outcomes differ from untested goal statements in that they have been validated. (See Appendixes B and E for more information on assessment materials and results.)

While the work of the Articulation and Achievement Project focused entirely on grades 7-14, and principally on French and Spanish teaching and learning, we believe that our methods and findings may have implications for other languages and for grades K-6, both for program development in those districts that are beginning to establish programs for younger children, and for those that already exist. At the very least, the methods employed by teachers and administrators in the Articulation and Achievement Project can be used to create and validate performance expectations for the early grades. Without further study, it is not possible to conclude that the Language Learning Continuum can be applied with equal confidence to programs that begin before grade 6. Nevertheless, for the increasing number of teachers and administrators studying the research landscape in order to set reasonable and attainable goals, the national Standards Sample Progress Indicators for grade 4, along with the descriptors for Stage I, may provide a starting point for ensuring that students develop well-rounded language skills in the early years, thus ensuring, to the degree possible, a firm footing for continued study. For this reason, while we do not attempt to make claims that extend beyond the scope of our work, we have taken the liberty of making suggestions that we believe may be useful to those exploring language programs for the K-6 population.

IMPROVING CURRICULUM AND INSTRUCTION IN YOUR SCHOOL

The purpose of this book is to provide practitioners and administrators with practical and realistic guidelines for building and improving standards-based foreign language programs. The Language Learning Continuum, a rich framework defining student performance goals, a central component of this book, combines the best practical classroom-based knowledge and experience with the demands of standards-based curriculum and sets high but attainable goals for all students. Furthermore, it provides a simple, straightforward basis for building curriculum that is independent of textbooks but can be used in conjunction with any published program. It can serve as an anchor for determining annual achievement goals for all students and for strengthening articulation from level to level, a critical component in overall student success. Finally, the Language Learning Continuum can help us realize the goal of the entire standards movement as described in Dennie Palmer Wolf's wager, to drive achievement up, to provide equitable access to worthwhile intellectual activities, and to reach widespread agreement about what we need to do together.

Chapter 2 describes the Language Learning Continuum in complete detail. In this chapter, the author describes each stage, gives samples of student work at each stage, and suggests which students typically fall into each category. In Chapter 3, the authors discuss the critical role of literature and culture in instruction and provide a context and rationale for de-emphasizing the perceived dichotomy between literature and language current in professional debate. The Language Learning Continuum contains little explicit direction about the role of either literature or culture in developing a well-balanced and effective program. This is not because the teachers who developed the continuum did not understand the importance of literature, art, and history, but rather because every attempt to fully encompass these topics resulted in a more prescriptive document than intended. By embedding the possibilities for integrating culture and literature into the curriculum within the continuum, language teachers have the opportunity to choose content and reading from an endless list of possibilities. Still, the importance of culture and literature in developing an effective language program that will produce well-rounded speakers, listeners, readers, and writers should not be underestimated. For this reason, Chapter 3 is devoted entirely to the integration of literature, art, and history at each stage of the Language Learning Continuum.

Chapter 4 fully addresses the questions raised by standardized testing and alternative assessment and the administration of performance assessments. A variety of methods of performance assessment applicable at each stage are outlined and the range of performance assessments, from portfolio to integrated assessments, are described. The samples provide a foundation for those wishing to use them as a basis for developing their own assessment tasks. Chapter 5 attempts to provide a context for future discussion and debate while suggesting strategies for moving forward.

Each chapter contains a separate section at the end entitled "Frequently Asked Questions." Over the course of the past four years, participants in the project have made presentations in their local districts, in their states, and at national conferences. They have kept a record of the questions most frequently asked at these events. Because these questions have arisen so often we have included them here, with answers, in the hope that they will respond to the questions readers may also have. Finally, we have included a bibliography that serves as a reference guide to the most informative works currently available for professional reading on this topic. While not intended to be exhaustive, it is a rich source for further reading and investigation.

FREQUENTLY ASKED QUESTIONS

What is the relationship between the Language Learning Continuum and the national standards document, *Standards for Foreign Language Learning: Preparing for the 21st Century?*

The *Standards for Foreign Language Learning* provide a clear and unified blueprint for the future of language education in the United States. Within the context of a K-12 foreign language program, the document outlines 11 content standards, suggesting student activities and providing classroom scenarios for attaining each of the standards at the elementary, middle, and high school levels.

In designing a curriculum, educators must translate standards into strategies for teaching, learning, and assessment, which are embedded in a clearly defined, well-articulated language learning sequence. Performance standards that answer the question "how good is good enough?" must also play a role in curriculum development. The Language Learning Continuum describes what a student should know and be able to do at five stages of achievement, provides samples of actual student work, and suggests tools for measuring student performance at each stage.

My state has its own detailed curriculum framework for foreign languages. How can I use it and the Language Learning Continuum at the same time—or should I?

A suggested approach is to examine your state's document in comparison to the Language Learning Continuum, and evaluate the state framework's usefulness in creating curricula and accompanying student assessments. The strength of the Language Learning Continuum lies in its realistic classroom-tested outcomes and performance assessments, which are built upon a clearly defined, well-articulated sequence of five stages of language study. These outcomes and assessment strategies may be more descriptive than those in a state document and can provide direction for translating a state document into curricula for actual classroom instruction.

How can the Language Learning Continuum help with placement after high school?

Many postsecondary institutions continue to base their placement of incoming students on either the number of completed years of high school language study or a placement test administered by the institution. In many cases, the placement does not accurately reflect a student's language ability.

As more foreign language educators and postsecondary admission personnel become familiar with the notion of performance outcomes, the potential exists to make known a student's abilities. For example, a high school student who has successfully completed Stage II in high school would be placed in a college/university course that encompasses Stage III knowledge and skills. Although no generally accepted vehicle currently exists to communicate student achievement levels in foreign language from high school to postsecondary institutions, there are some possibilities that could be considered. For example, a standard notation of a student's completed stage included on the high school transcript would be a simple and practical solution to the problems associated with student placement.

REFERENCES

National Standards in Foreign Language Education Project. 1996. *Standards for Foreign Language Learning: Preparing for the 21st Century.* Yonkers, NY: The National Standards in Foreign Language Education Project.

Wolf, Dennie P. 1994. "Curriculum and Assessment Standards: Common Measures or Conversations?" In *The Future of Education: Perspectives on National Standards in America*, edited by Nina Cobb. New York: College Entrance Examination Board, 85-106.

LANGUAGE LEARNING CONTINUUM
STAGE I

FUNCTION

Students develop the ability to:

- greet and respond to greetings;
- introduce and respond to introductions;
- engage in conversations;
- express likes and dislikes;
- make requests;
- obtain information;
- understand some ideas and familiar details;
- begin to provide information.

CONTEXT

Students can perform these functions:

- when speaking, in face-to-face social interaction;
- when listening, in social interaction and using audio or video texts;
- when reading, using authentic materials, e.g., menus, photos, posters, schedules, charts, signs, and short narratives;
- when writing notes, lists, poems, postcards, and short letters.

TEXT TYPE

Students can:

- use short sentences, learned words and phrases, and simple questions and commands when speaking and writing;
- understand some ideas and familiar details presented in clear, uncomplicated speech when listening;
- understand short texts enhanced by visual clues when reading.

ACCURACY

Students:

- communicate effectively with some hesitation and errors, which do not hinder comprehension;
- demonstrate culturally acceptable behavior for Stage I functions;
- understand most important information.

CONTENT

Stages I and II often include some combination of the following topics:

- **the self:** family, friends, home, rooms, health, school, schedules, leisure activities, campus life, likes and dislikes, shopping, clothes, prices, size and quantity, and pets and animals.
- **beyond self:** geography, topography, directions, buildings and monuments, weather and seasons, symbols, cultural and historical figures, places and events, colors, numbers, days, dates, months, time, food and customs, transportation, travel, and professions and work.

LANGUAGE LEARNING CONTINUUM
STAGE II

FUNCTION	CONTEXT	TEXT TYPE
Students expand their ability to perform all the functions developed in Stage I. They also develop the ability to: ■ make requests; ■ express their needs; ■ understand and express important ideas and some detail; ■ describe and compare; ■ use and understand expressions indicating emotion.	*Students can perform these functions:* ■ when speaking, in face-to-face social interaction; ■ when listening, in social interaction and using audio or video texts; ■ when reading, using authentic materials, e.g., short narratives, advertisements, tickets, brochures, and other media; ■ when writing letters and short guided compositions.	*Students can:* ■ use and understand learned expressions, sentences, and strings of sentences, questions, and polite commands when speaking and listening; ■ create simple paragraphs when writing; ■ understand important ideas and some details in highly contextualized authentic texts when reading.

ACCURACY

Students:

■ demonstrate increasing fluency and control of vocabulary;
■ show no significant pattern of error when performing Stage I functions;
■ communicate effectively with some pattern of error, which may interfere slightly with full comprehension when performing Stage II functions;
■ understand oral and written discourse, with few errors in comprehension when reading; demonstrate culturally appropriate behavior for Stage II functions.

CONTENT

Stages I and II often include some combination of the following topics:

■ **the self:** family, friends, home, rooms, health, school, schedules, leisure activities, campus life, likes and dislikes, shopping, clothes, prices, size and quantity, and pets and animals.

■ **beyond self:** geography, topography, directions, buildings and monuments, weather and seasons, symbols, cultural and historical figures, places and events, colors, numbers, days, dates, months, time, food and customs, transportation, travel, and professions and work.

LANGUAGE LEARNING CONTINUUM
STAGE III

FUNCTION	CONTEXT	TEXT TYPE
Students expand their ability to perform all the functions developed in Stages I and II. They also develop the ability to:	*Students can perform these functions:*	*Students can:*

FUNCTION

Students expand their ability to perform all the functions developed in Stages I and II. They also develop the ability to:

- clarify and ask for and comprehend clarification;
- express and understand opinions;
- narrate and understand narration in the present, past, and future;
- identify, state, and understand feelings and emotions.

CONTEXT

Students can perform these functions:

- when speaking, in face-to-face social interaction and in simple transactions on the phone;
- when listening, in social interaction and using audio or video texts;
- when reading short stories, poems, essays, and articles;
- when writing journals, letters, and essays.

TEXT TYPE

Students can:

- use strings of related sentences when speaking;
- understand most spoken language when the message is deliberately and carefully conveyed by a speaker accustomed to dealing with learners when listening;
- create simple paragraphs when writing;
- acquire knowledge and new information from comprehensive, authentic texts when reading.

ACCURACY
Students:

- tend to become less accurate as the task or message becomes more complex, and some patterns of error may interfere with meaning;
- generally choose appropriate vocabulary for familiar topics, but as the complexity of the message increases, there is evidence of hesitation and groping for words, as well as patterns of mispronunciation and intonation;
- generally use culturally appropriate behavior in social situations;
- are able to understand and retain most key ideas and some supporting detail when reading and listening.

CONTENT
Content includes cultural, personal, and social topics such as:

- history, art, literature, music, current affairs, and civilization, with an emphasis on significant people and events in these fields;
- career choices, the environment, social issues, and political issues.

LANGUAGE LEARNING CONTINUUM
STAGE IV

FUNCTION

Students expand their ability to perform all the functions developed in Stages I, II, and III. They also develop the ability to:

- give and understand advice and suggestions;
- initiate, engage in, and close a conversation;
- compare and contrast;
- explain and support an opinion.

CONTEXT

Students can perform these functions:

- when speaking, in face-to-face social interaction, in simple transactions on the phone, and in group discussions, prepared debates, and presentations;
- when listening, in social interaction and using audio or video texts, including TV interviews and newscasts;
- when reading short literary texts, poems, and articles;
- when writing journals, letters, and essays.

TEXT TYPE

Students can:

- use simple discourse in a series of coherent paragraphs when speaking;
- understand most authentic spoken language when listening;
- create a series of coherent paragraphs when writing;
- acquire knowledge and new information from comprehensive, authentic texts when reading.

ACCURACY
Students:

- can engage in conversations with few significant patterns of error and use a wide range of appropriate vocabulary;
- demonstrate a heightened awareness of culturally appropriate behavior, although, as the task or message becomes more complex, they tend to become less accurate;
- are able to understand and report most key ideas and some supporting detail when reading and listening.

CONTENT
Content embraces:

- concepts of broader cultural significance, including institutions such as the education system, the government, and political and social issues in the target culture;
- topics of social and personal interest such as music, literature, the arts, and the sciences.

LANGUAGE LEARNING CONTINUUM
STAGE V

FUNCTION

Students expand their ability to perform all the functions developed in Stages I, II, III, and IV. They also develop the ability to:

- conduct transactions and negotiations;
- substantiate and elaborate opinions;
- convince and persuade;
- analyze and critique.

CONTEXT

- Students can perform these functions in almost any context, including many complex situations.

TEXT TYPE

- Students can perform these functions in extended discourse when appropriate.

ACCURACY

Students:

- use culturally appropriate language, characterized by a wide range of vocabulary, with few patterns of error, although speech may contain some hesitation and normal pauses;
- comprehend significant ideas and most supporting details.

CONTENT

Content embraces:

- concepts of broader cultural significance, including social issues in the target culture, such as the environment and human rights;
- abstract ideas concerning art, literature, politics, and society.

CHAPTER 2

THE LANGUAGE LEARNING CONTINUUM

C hapter 1 described the major lessons learned over the course of the Articulation and Achievement Project in the context of national standards and the call for greater accountability in the educational domain. In this chapter, complete descriptions of the student performance outcomes in the Language Learning Continuum are provided. These outcomes may be adapted to the circumstances in a particular school or district in order to improve articulation, avoid repetition, validate prior student learning, and provide students with a clear understanding of their progress, thus engaging them more fully in the learning process. As pointed out in Chapter 1, progress from one course to another in language study has most often been determined by the learner's "seat time" rather than by any definitive measure of competence in the language. Experience tells us, however, that successful language acquisition is the result of a combination of complex factors. When teachers fully understand this, they will find it easier to work with students who have a variety of strengths and weaknesses, simply by knowing what the strengths and weaknesses are. While planning programs based on this knowledge and creating classes where students are able to successfully meet the goals described before moving on to the next "level" is an ideal solution, it is often, at least in the current structure of most secondary schools, not practical. But experienced teachers, armed with a basic understanding of the measurable factors of student performance when the school year begins, can plan lessons, develop assessments, and design portfolio activities to meet and match individual student needs.

The Language Learning Continuum defines student progress along a learning progression that is independent of textbooks, independent of individual programs and schedules, and independent of available resources. It is a continuum that may be used to guide any program since it uses clear objectives to transform topic- and structure-based curricula and instruction into a coherent and realizable performance-based model. It describes what students should know and be able to do as a result of foreign language study. Using a five-stage structure, it defines standards in terms of performance rather than achievement. It provides a basis for more fully articulated programs, particularly at the important transitional stages between middle and high school and between high school and college. Ultimately, the Language Learning Continuum is intended to replace what many foreign language teachers now consider the expected student outcomes for levels 1, 2, 3, 4, and 5 in grades 7-12, and beginning, intermediate, and advanced courses at the postsecondary level.

STAGES IN LEARNING A SECOND LANGUAGE

Searching for a term to describe the performance level of students tested in a wide and diverse array of schools, project participants decided upon the word "stage" in order to avoid confusion with terms like "level." "Stage" highlights the fact that, in spite of wide discrepancies in the number of years of study, different students, in different schools with similar programs, knew and were able to perform specific real-life linguistic tasks at similar performance levels when tested. This led to the belief that if student progress were reported in terms of "stage" rather than "level" or "year," and if courses were designed using realistic parameters based on previous performance, the task of ensuring smooth articulation and, ultimately, of improving student success and confidence, would be greatly facilitated.

In order to design and implement a second-language program defined by performance rather than by time on task or topics covered, it is important to understand that there are no perfect solutions. Learning a new language is complex. Individual students in the same class with similar learning profiles progress at different rates, slowing down at times and speeding ahead at others. Moreover, experience has taught us that students with similar learning profiles vary greatly in the rate at which they acquire another language. When you add age, maturity, motivation, language experience, resources, and quality of instruction into the mix, it is easy to see why it is possible for students of similar age and grade level to perform at different stages, even though they are in the same class.

The Language Learning Continuum is organized using concepts derived from the ACTFL *Proficiency Guidelines*: function, context, text type, accuracy, and content. The following explanations may serve as a useful cross-reference when studying the Continuum.

- **Function**: what a student can do with the language at a given stage. Functions are specific language-based tasks normally performed in the course of daily life, such as relating an event, giving advice, reading for information, listening to a news report, and communicating ideas in writing.

- **Context**: the settings in which students can reasonably be expected to perform the functions described for a given stage. Context refers to the settings or situations in which a particular function may take place. For example, greeting and leave-taking generally occur in the context of a face-to-face meeting and conversation. Context provides a delivery system, answering the questions: "where?" "when?" and "with whom?"

- **Text type**: the structure of written or spoken language as it occurs at various stages in students' language development. In the Language Learning Continuum, text type refers to the kind of sentence structures students normally use at a given stage. While exceptions occur, typical students progress from single words and short phrases to sentences and paragraphs. Naturally, the age of students and their level of sophistication in the use of their primary language is a significant factor in the consideration of text type.

- **Accuracy:** the degree to which student performance is structurally and sociolinguistically correct. Accuracy is the term that qualifies the linguistic behavior of language learners and answers "how well?" Sociolinguistic factors, vocabulary, syntax, pronunciation, and fluency interact closely in the consideration of accuracy, and all play an important role.

- **Content:** the subjects about which a student at a given stage is able to communicate. Content refers to the relative complexity of the information understood or conveyed by learners—what topics of discussion students are able to understand, and talk and write about. Examples include familiar topics such as school and family, as well as more advanced topics such as current events, history, art, and literature. Content is the substance of communication.

THE LANGUAGE LEARNING CONTINUUM: WHAT IT MEANS AND HOW IT WORKS

STAGE I

Stage I begins when a student starts to learn a second language. While further research will be required to establish the validity of the Stage I competencies for programs that begin earlier than sixth or seventh grade, the nature of the descriptions are general enough to serve as an excellent starting point. Stage I may occur at any age; it may encompass a four- to five-year sequence that begins in the elementary or middle school, a one- to two-year high school program, or a one- to two-semester college or university program. In the Articulation and Achievement Project, the majority of students whose performance met or exceeded the standards of Stage I typically fit the following descriptions:

1. Students at the end of the eighth grade enrolled in middle school programs (seventh and eighth grade) that provided between 160 and 200 minutes per week of instruction.

2. Students whose language study began in high school and who were at the end of their first year when assessed. (Note: In general, most of these students did not perform as well as the students described above. Language use was less fluid and vocabulary acquisition less broad.)

3. Students whose language study began in high school and who were in the fall of their second year of language instruction at the time the assessment was given.

While Stage I is the most basic stage, it is also the most important; it lays the critical foundation for all future classroom-based language instruction. Instruction at this stage must be balanced, requiring students to learn the "basics" while encouraging them at the same time to use what they have learned in important ways. In his book, *Assessing Student Performance* (1990), Grant Wiggins points out the need to ask students to engage in "worthwhile intellectual activities" similar to those activities engaged in by real people in the real world and to produce rather than reproduce knowledge. By adhering to these principles, and focusing on the practice of the functions described as appropriate to this stage, teachers can help students remain committed to the effort required to successfully pass through Stages I and II and to enter successfully into Stage III and beyond, where they are fully able to "produce" their own thoughts and ideas in the target language.

In the diverse school settings involved in the Articulation and Achievement Project, Stage I is, by and large, the domain of early adolescence—grades 6, 7, 8, and 9. For language teachers who understand that students of this age need to feel increasingly independent and competent, Stage I offers real challenges. How can we reinforce and encourage student growth and development into young adulthood when the ability to use the language learned is so limited? First, we need to understand that the notion of Stage I as limited is false. While it is true that Stage I learners do not have control over broad content, they do develop many of the skills that adult speakers use regularly in daily life. Taking the time to review with students what these skills are and what they will lead to over time will help young learners to be patient with themselves and, more important, to be patient with the process required to develop them. It is also important to plan classroom activities and portfolio assignments that are as closely aligned to real-life behaviors as possible. Lists of "Things to Do Tomorrow" make more sense than simple lists of infinitives; role-playing in contexts that reflect real life makes more sense than memorizing impersonal dialogues. In a word, an important aspect of maintaining student interest is the degree to which we are able to connect instruction to meaningful and worthwhile activities. Appendix C contains a wide variety of appropriate activities that can be altered and revised according to individual teacher preference and used in numerous ways to achieve this goal.

LANGUAGE LEARNING CONTINUUM
STAGE I

FUNCTION

Students develop the ability to:

- greet and respond to greetings;
- introduce and respond to introductions;
- engage in conversations;
- express likes and dislikes;
- make requests;
- obtain information;
- understand some ideas and familiar details;
- begin to provide information.

CONTEXT

Students can perform these functions:

- when speaking, in face-to-face social interaction;
- when listening, in social interaction and using audio or video texts;
- when reading, using authentic materials, e.g., menus, photos, posters, schedules, charts, signs, and short narratives;
- when writing notes, lists, poems, postcards, and short letters.

TEXT TYPE

Students can:

- use short sentences, learned words and phrases, and simple questions and commands when speaking and writing;
- understand some ideas and familiar details presented in clear, uncomplicated speech when listening;
- understand short texts enhanced by visual clues when reading.

ACCURACY

Students:

- communicate effectively with some hesitation and errors, which do not hinder comprehension;
- demonstrate culturally acceptable behavior for Stage I functions;
- understand most important information.

CONTENT

Stages I and II often include some combination of the following topics:

- **the self:** family, friends, home, rooms, health, school, schedules, leisure activities, campus life, likes and dislikes, shopping, clothes, prices, size and quantity, and pets and animals.
- **beyond self:** geography, topography, directions, buildings and monuments, weather and seasons, symbols, cultural and historical figures, places and events, colors, numbers, days, dates, months, time, food and customs, transportation, travel, and professions and work.

In order to provide concrete examples of what Stage I performance "looks like," we have included below one sample of written student work from each of the three categories used to describe student performance: (3) Exceeds Expectation, (2) Meets Expectation, and (1) Falls Below Expectation. (See full explanation on pp. 100-107.)

Each of the samples falls within the parameters defined by Stage I for function, context, text type, accuracy, and content. The students whose work is shown here were given 25 minutes to consider what they were going to write, to write it, and to review and revise it, if necessary. They were responding to the following prompt:

Write a postcard to your pen pal in Puerto Rico. Tell him/her that your close friend is going to travel there during the school vacation. Describe your friend. You may want to write about age, appearance, likes, and dislikes. You may also add any information about your friend that you think your pen pal will find interesting.

Please note that these student samples are not error free. They are reproduced here exactly as they were written. The original text was handwritten but is word processed here to facilitate reading. As you read each sample refer back to the appropriate stage performance expectations to determine why students received the score they did.

SAMPLE 1 EXCEEDS EXPECTATION

Querido Amanda,

Cómo estás? Estoy muy bien, pero muy ocupada. En un mes, mi amigo David va a viajar en Puerto Rico por sus vacaciones de colegio. David tiene quince años. Es muy alto y delgado con pelo rubio, corto y lacio. Tiene lentes pero no tiene barba o bigote. David es inteligente, simpático y divertido. Le gusta jugar al tenis, andar en bicicleta, y leer. No a le gusta ver la televisión. Tiene dos hermanos, Duane y Jamie, y una hermana, Carmen. Habla español muy bien. Sé que tu y David van a divertirles.

XXXXXXX

Hola José,

¿Comó estás? Yo estoy escribiendo para decirte de mi buen amigo, Juan. Piensa visitar a Puerto Rico en el verano. Entonces, yo gusta presentar te sobre su visita. También, yo gusto a describir él a tú ese él; el es alto y blanco. El tiene diecisiete años. Entre de mis amigos, él es inteligente. Él le encanta jugar la música en la casa, pero encanta en el conciertos mucho. La playa es muy bien para él. Él también gusta jugar el beísbol con las amigos. Yo espero tú disfrutas el tan tu buen amigo.

Hasta luego,
XXXXXXX

hola José

Yo estoy escribiendo tu decir qui mi amigo ~~es au va soy~~ es a visitar en el veirano llegar el seis de mayo. El es alto, moreno, y me gusta deportes. El tambian gusta va la ~~part~~ fiesta.

Tu amigo,
XXXXXXX

STAGE II

Stage II is, in many ways, directly related to Stage I in that students are not yet fully capable of using language to express their own ideas precisely, to read what most interests them, or to understand everything they would like to read or hear. It is a progression in terms of gradually increasing vocabulary acquisition, fluency, aural and reading comprehension, and sophistication in written and oral expression. The Stage II student may be in middle or high school at the traditional levels 1, 2, or 3, or a college or university student in a second-semester course. In our experience, while many students who had begun language study in grade 7 met the Stage II expectations in the fall of the tenth grade, those who had begun later, for example in grade 9, did not reach this stage until the spring of grade 10 or early in grade 11. At the postsecondary level, students often reached Stage II at the end of the second semester.

Like Stage I, Stage II builds on students' growing awareness of the world and encourages learning skills that will enable them to work and live in the world as it becomes increasingly multilingual. By the end of Stage II, students will have acquired much more "language power." They have expanded their ability to perform all the functions developed earlier and have added new functions that lead them closer to having more freedom to say exactly what they want to say, rather than being limited by learned expressions. At this stage, students gain confidence, perform Stage I functions with ease, and are better able to demonstrate culturally appropriate behaviors. The content of Stages I and II is nearly interchangeable and often determined by the materials teachers use in instruction.

An interesting insight gained as a result of the study of so many student samples between 1993 and 1996 is that at Stage II, comprehension, both aural and reading, increases rapidly and the rate of growth in these areas seems to outstrip parallel growth in interpersonal and presentation skills. While patterns of error can be seen mainly in newly acquired structures, students tend to neglect previously learned structures and often need to be reminded that skills learned earlier are useful and necessary for expanding linguistic competence.

In order to provide concrete examples of what Stage II performance "looks like," we have included below one sample of written student work from each of the three categories used to describe student performance: (3) Exceeds Expectation, (2) Meets Expectation, and (1) Falls Below Expectation. (See full explanation on pp. 100-107.) Each of the samples falls within the parameters defined by Stage II for function, context, text type, accuracy, and content. The students whose work is shown here were given 25 minutes to consider what they were going to write, to write it, and to review and revise, if necessary. They were responding to the following prompt:

Write a short letter to your pen pal in Canada. Tell him/her that your close friend is going to travel there during the school vacation. Describe your friend as fully as possible. You may want to write about age,

LANGUAGE LEARNING CONTINUUM
STAGE II

FUNCTION

Students expand their ability to perform all the functions developed in Stage I. They also develop the ability to:

- make requests;
- express their needs;
- understand and express important ideas and some detail;
- describe and compare;
- use and understand expressions indicating emotion.

CONTEXT

Students can perform these functions:

- when speaking, in face-to-face social interaction;
- when listening, in social interaction and using audio or video texts;
- when reading, using authentic materials, e.g., short narratives, advertisements, tickets, brochures, and other media;
- when writing letters and short guided compositions.

TEXT TYPE

Students can:

- use and understand learned expressions, sentences, and strings of sentences, questions, and polite commands when speaking and listening;
- create simple paragraphs when writing;
- understand important ideas and some details in highly contextualized authentic texts when reading.

ACCURACY

Students:

- demonstrate increasing fluency and control of vocabulary;
- show no significant pattern of error when performing Stage I functions;
- communicate effectively with some pattern of error, which may interfere slightly with full comprehension when performing Stage II functions;
- understand oral and written discourse, with few errors in comprehension when reading; demonstrate culturally appropriate behavior for Stage II functions.

CONTENT

Stages I and II often include some combination of the following topics:

- **the self:** family, friends, home, rooms, health, school, schedules, leisure activities, campus life, likes and dislikes, shopping, clothes, prices, size and quantity, and pets and animals.
- **beyond self:** geography, topography, directions, buildings and monuments, weather and seasons, symbols, cultural and historical figures, places and events, colors, numbers, days, dates, months, time, food and customs, transportation, travel, and professions and work.

appearance, likes and dislikes. You may also add any information about your friend that you think your pen pal will find interesting.

Please note that these student samples are not error free. They are reproduced here exactly as they were written. The original text was handwritten but is word processed here to facilitate reading. As you read each sample refer back to the appropriate stage performance expectations to determine why students received the score they did.

SAMPLE 1 EXCEEDS EXPECTATION

Chère Caroline,
Salut! Ça va? Je vais bien. Mon ami Jacques ira au Canada cet été. Il a dix neuf ans, il est blonde, et il est très sympathique. Il aime jouer au sports - le foot, le volley, le basket, et il joue bien au tennis. Il veut faire du camping au Canada. Est-ce que tu sais un bon place? Il veut faire du marche à pied, faire d l'alpinisme, et faire de la natation mais il n'aime pas la plage et la mer. Il aime nager au lac. Peut-être, Jacques ira au parc près de ta maison, et tu pourras faire de reconnaissance d'eux. Si tu fais de reconnaissance de Jacques tu aimeras beaucoup! Est-ce que tu as un amour? Jacques adore la musique classique! Écrire-moi et dis-moi si Jacques aimera le parc près de ta maison. Á bientôt!

Amicalement,
XXXXXXXXXX

SAMPLE 2 MEETS EXPECTATION

Cher Jean-Luc,
Bonjour, commo ça va. Ici, ça va biein. Le temps ici est beau. Mon amie Jason ~~est~~ fait a voyager au Canada. Il est grand mais moins grand que mon frère. Il aime le rouge, vert, noir, et blanc. Il parle ~~boa~~ bien français et espanol. Il adore vertes chemises et noir et blanc jeans. Il ~~joue~~ aime jouer au basketball et au football. Il n'aime pas jouer ~~de~~ au tennis. Il mange trois pommes de la semaine. Il déstese parler au téléphone. Mais, il adore chanter pour filles. Il a ~~quai~~ quatorze ans. Il est blond, sympa, amusant, et tres sportif. Il ne porte jamais violets vêtements. Il deteste aller au cinema. Il adore ~~ma~~ sa mere et sa soeur. Il est tres content homme.

Amities,
XXXXXXX

Chère Maria,

Bonjour Ça va? Ça va bien ici à . . . . Ma amie Olga va la vacation au Canada. Elle est americaine et parle françe et angle. Elle est 17 ans. Elle est intelligante. Elle est petite et brune. Ell aime porte le tee-shirt et le blue jeens avec les baskets. Elle est sympa une fille. Olga est entousiate pour les sports. Elle n'pas aime parle au telephone. Elle n'pas dormere à la maison. Elle aime regarde la télè. Olga aime mange une pizza et salades et fruits. Elle aime jouie avec une chien. Elle aime alle au parc. Au-revoir.

STAGE III

The development of the Stage III performance expectations proved to be, by far, the most interesting and revealing work of the entire project. In studying samples of student work, oral and written, most of our assumptions about these "intermediate" students were proven false. In addition, we realized that, to our knowledge, none of the characteristics that we found prevalent in hundreds of samples had ever been described before. Here is an overview of what we learned and how what we learned may apply directly to changing second language instruction.

Stage III is a pivotal stage, as students move from the comfort of learned material to the challenging world of consistently creating their own meaning using the language they are learning. Students at this stage are beginning to adapt vocabulary to their needs and to pursue their own interests in the language. They are struggling to become independent users of the language. As the repertoire of vocabulary and structures increases, and as their ability to read, hear, and understand more of the target language grows, students both want and are asked to attempt more complex and original tasks. College-level Stage III students may well possess a wider base of experience and broader knowledge of history, culture, literature, art, and language, as well as a more highly developed sense of independence and self-reliance than high school students. Nevertheless, in general, college-age students at Stage III do not possess greater linguistic capacities by virtue of being older and more mature.

Within Stage III, learners possess very different backgrounds and profiles. At the high school level, many have successfully completed first- and second-year courses (grades 7-10), while at the college level, students enter Stage III by several routes—most commonly from beginning college or university courses or by having completed three or four years of high school study. However, some students enter Stage III courses with other backgrounds, which may include:

- an extended sequence of language instruction that began in elementary or middle school,
- immersion or intensive programs in the United States and/or other countries, and
- a home background in the language chosen for study.

What we learned over the course of three years, in case after case, with students at both the secondary and postsecondary levels, was that as the knowledge band widens and the potential to express themselves grows, the ability to do so with the same level of accuracy as they demonstrated in Stages I and II often decreases. Students are often unable to organize and coordinate everything they know. Ideas and feelings spill out in a rather unpredictable fashion, sometimes leading teachers to wonder whether students have learned anything in the first few years of language study.

The students assessed at Stage III during this project, principally students in the third or fourth year of high school or in the third and fourth semester of college study, failed to perform as well as their teachers had predicted. Although students had demonstrated their knowledge of the rules and structure of the language in typical testing formats and were reading materials appropriate to their level of study, they were simply unable to put it all together when asked to speak and write in an unrehearsed performance format. Discussion among project participants and colleagues in their schools and colleges revealed that many of these students were motivated and willing learners, but that the need to "cover" a certain number of concepts and materials before the end of the school year could leave many of them behind. A significant number would either drop language study altogether or move on, often unprepared for the demands of the next level. Through the process of student evaluation and assessment, project participants learned firsthand the meaning of the developmental nature of language acquisition. They also learned that successfully meeting the criteria for Stage III requires more than the traditional third-year high school course, or third- or fourth-semester college study. The implications of this finding are far-reaching.

Question: If accuracy is an overriding factor in determining students' grades, won't some students going through this period in their development become discouraged and eventually give up?

Answer: Yes, we think so. If, as the *Standards* suggest, language study is necessary and appropriate for every student, courses should be redesigned to allow the majority of students to master the outcomes described in Stage III. We now believe that this factor may be a critical one in understanding why so many students typically give up at exactly this stage in their language education.

Not to be overlooked, at least at the college level, is the fact that many students complete the language requirement at the end of the third or fourth semester and choose not to continue. Further research is needed to understand why this happens.

In order to provide concrete examples of what Stage III "looks like," we have included below one sample of written student work from each of the three categories used to describe student performance: (3) Exceeds Expectation, (2) Meets Expectation, and (1) Falls Below Expectation. (See full explanation on pp. 100-107.) Each of the samples falls within the parameters defined by Stage III for function, context, text type, accuracy, and content. The students whose work is shown here were given 40 minutes to consider what they were going to write, to write it, and to review and revise, if necessary. The open-

LANGUAGE LEARNING CONTINUUM
STAGE III

FUNCTION	CONTEXT	TEXT TYPE
Students expand their ability to perform all the functions developed in Stages I and II. They also develop the ability to:	*Students can perform these functions:*	*Students can:*
■ clarify and ask for and comprehend clarification;	■ when speaking, in face-to-face social interaction and in simple transactions on the phone;	■ use strings of related sentences when speaking;
■ express and understand opinions;	■ when listening, in social interaction and using audio or video texts;	■ understand most spoken language when the message is deliberately and carefully conveyed by a speaker accustomed to dealing with learners when listening;
■ narrate and understand narration in the present, past, and future;	■ when reading short stories, poems, essays, and articles;	■ create simple paragraphs when writing;
■ identify, state, and understand feelings and emotions.	■ when writing journals, letters, and essays.	■ acquire knowledge and new information from comprehensive, authentic texts when reading.

ACCURACY
Students:

- ■ tend to become less accurate as the task or message becomes more complex, and some patterns of error may interfere with meaning;
- ■ generally choose appropriate vocabulary for familiar topics, but as the complexity of the message increases, there is evidence of hesitation and groping for words, as well as patterns of mispronunciation and intonation;
- ■ generally use culturally appropriate behavior in social situations;
- ■ are able to understand and retain most key ideas and some supporting detail when reading and listening.

CONTENT
Content includes cultural, personal, and social topics such as:

- ■ history, art, literature, music, current affairs, and civilization, with an emphasis on significant people and events in these fields;
- ■ career choices, the environment, social issues, and political issues.

ended nature of this prompt allows students to respond using their own ideas. The prompt was:

You have met your ideal friend. Write a journal entry telling in as much detail as possible what the person is like and why you like him or her.

In the student samples below, provided in both French and Spanish, please note the kinds of errors students made, remembering that these students had all successfully passed through the first, second, and sometimes the third year of language study prior to taking this performance assessment.

Please note that these student samples are not error free. They are reproduced here exactly as they were written. The original text was handwritten but is word processed here to facilitate reading. As you read each sample refer back to the appropriate stage performance expectations to determine why students received the score they did.

SAMPLE 1 EXCEEDS EXPECTATION (SPANISH)

Encontré mi amiga ideal hoy. Ella es muy alta y tiene pelo moreno. Pero su aparencia no es importante. Su personalidad es importante. Mi amiga ideal es muy simpática. Ella siempre es allí cuando yo necesito hablar con ella. Mi amiga ideal es muy cómica también. Ella tiene un sentido del humor.

Nos gusta hacer los cosas iguales. Nos gustan la musica, los bailes, y ir al cine. Nouetra cosa favorita es ir de compras. Nos gusta comprar cosas nuevas.

La característica mejor de mi amigo es su honestad. Ella siempre me dice la verdad. Le digo la verdad. Le digo la verdad a ella también. Mi amiga ideal es mi amiga mejor también. Se llama XXXXXXX.

SAMPLE 1 EXCEEDS EXPECTATION (FRENCH)

Il fait presque deux mois que j'ai fait la connaissance de Marc. Il fait de la photographie comme son travail, et il joue de la batterie aussi dans un group de la musique rock-a-billy à Manhattan. Toutes les deux nous aimons la musique des années '50, surtout la musique d'Elvis Presley. Marc est petit pour un homme, mais avec beaucoup des muscles—comme un nageur. Il a de la cheveux brun et les yeux verts. Il porte des bottes noirs en cuire et il aime les jeans noir. Il a une visage très belle et un corps en très bonne forme physique. Il est aussi intelligent; il aime particulièremant discuter de la politique et de la religion. Pendant deux ans il travaillait pour un groupe politique à Chicago. Il est assez serieux dans toutes les choses qu'il fait dans la vie.

Il a eu de la chance parce qu'il peut voyager beaucoup dans son travail, et il aime les langues étrangers. Nous pouvons parler toute la nuit, sept jours á la semaine....mais il toujours me fait des surprises. L'autre jour quand je suis retournée de l'université Marc m'avait fait de la cuisine extraordinaire. Il est comme ça - genereux. Maintenant je suis en train d'apprendre jouer de la guittare et Marc me donne des leçons. Nous allons former un groupe de la musique cuand je suis assez bonne en jouant de la guittare. Je n'ai jamais fait la connaissance d'une persone comme lui. Il est intelligent, il comprend l'humeur, il est, pour moi au moins, le plus beau homme du monde, et il veut être avec moi. Tout le temps il me donne de la courage pour faire des choses nouveaux et il me dit que je peux les faire. Marc exude de la confiance et moi, j'aime ça.

SAMPLE 2   MEETS EXPECTATION (SPANISH)

El verano pasado fue el primera vez que veí mi amig favorita. Nosotros estuvimos en el oeste de los Estados Unidos donde andamos en el montaña todos los días. Ella sonríe casi todo el tiempo. Cuando ella está triste ella es una optimista. Por eso, siempre yo río cuando yo estoy con ella. Ella es muy generosa también. La semana pasada nosotros estuvimos en una tienda. Allí, yo veía un dibujo de una vaca que me gusté mucho. Cuando no veí, ella me compró el dibujo. Me gusta cuando ella me sorpresa, proque ella siempre es creativo y inteligente. Ella es muy simpática a todo el mundo. Un día, ella le ayudaba un hombre que no veí en la calle. Muchas veces ella me ayuda con mi tarea proque ella sabe mucho sobre todos de los clases. Ella no le importa que otras personas creen sobre ella; un cualidad que yo admiro mucho. Ella tiene muchos culidades importantes. Ella es responsable, simpática, madura, generosa y más. Elll ha estado mi amiga para un tiempo largo.

Elle s'appelle Michelle et elle est ma meilleure amie. Elle a beaucoup de problems avec sa famille alors elle est toujours dans chez moi. Maintenant elle a un petit ami alors elle est avec lui quelquefois. Elle regarde comme moi et beaucoup de persons ont demandé nous si elle est ma soeure. Elle est petite et elle est brune et elle a beaucoup de cheveux. Elle est très intelligent et elle a toujours une bonne note. Elle aime la musique et l'art beaucoup. Elle chants bien et elle est une bonne artiste! Aussi elle aime le formage et elle le mange toujours. Elle n'aime pas faire du shopping mais elle a beaucoup de vetements et choses. Comme moi elle joue l'hockey sur la gazon. Nous sommes allées en France et elle a parlé français très bien. Nous aimons regarder les matchs dons la télé et nous aimons ecouter la musique. Elle est ma meilleure amie et je pense que elle seras ma meilleur amie pour toujours.

Me gusta un amigo o una amiga para cuando ellos ser a otros personas. Mi amigo gustaria hacer muchas cosas con mi y nuestro amigos. El escala unos mountaños con mi y en fin de semaña noces pudemos mirar a televisor. El piensa cuanto el sentir. Mi amigo no beber calveza mucho pero vive para divirtido. El siempre escuchar musica y gustar ir a fiestas en fin de semaña o ir una pelicula con otros amigos.
Mi idealistico amigo piensa sobre su amigos y amigas.

Voila mon amie. Il s'appelle Pierre. Il est grande, mais je suis plus grande que Pierre. J'ai vu Pierre jouer le baseball contre l'equipe de moi. Pendant le match, il courir a moi parce-que je suis le catcher et nous a frappons. Et de sa jour, nous sommes amie. Pierre est tres timid, mais tres curieux. J'aime Pierre quand il me donne son voiture pour un jour. Il m'ensigné a conduct le voiture. Il est tres interessante, l'étè passé il a recontree un travail pour moi. Il est un vrai ami quand j'ai besoin d'une personne, il est le personne que m'aide. Dans l'ecole qui Il va, il a prendre du français aussi. Quelquefois, nous parlons en française. Mais, je suis plus intelligent.

Stage IV

Once having emerged from the complexities of Stage III, students begin to develop, enhance, and extend their knowledge and skills. Stage IV students tend to be risk-takers, willing to make mistakes and to self-correct. These students explore topics that are less familiar, experiment with more complex structures associated with advanced functions, and engage in more elaborate, extended, and well-organized discourse. Stage IV students have made great and measurable strides in oral expression and listening comprehension. Their written work may be nearly free of errors; they can read and understand relatively sophisticated texts. They perform with greater confidence, fewer hesitations, and quicker self-correction; they are skilled at circumlocution and have a tendency to show persistence when they want to get an idea across. Stage IV students react more quickly and accurately to a speaker with native ability; their interpersonal dialogue is more naturally paced and authentic.

Students who achieve Stage IV outcomes are likely to have completed four to six years of middle and high school foreign language study, or five to eight semesters of college or university study. Additionally, these students may have spent significant time in a country where the target language is spoken.

In order to provide concrete examples of what Stage IV performance "looks like," we have included below one sample in French of written student work from each of the three categories used to describe student performance: (3) Exceeds Expectation, (2) Meets Expectation, and (1) Falls Below Expectation. (See full explanation on pp. 100-107.) Each of the samples falls within the parameters defined by Stage IV for function, context, text type, accuracy, and content. The students whose work is shown here were given 40 minutes to consider what they were going to write, to write it, and to review and revise it, if necessary. The prompt was:

> **Your friend asks you to write a letter of reference recommending him/her for a position as a camp counselor in Quebec for 8- to 10-year-old campers. A good letter of reference usually includes information about how**

LANGUAGE LEARNING CONTINUUM
STAGE IV

FUNCTION

Students expand their ability to perform all the functions developed in Stages I, II, and III. They also develop the ability to:

- give and understand advice and suggestions;
- initiate, engage in, and close a conversation;
- compare and contrast;
- explain and support an opinion.

CONTEXT

Students can perform these functions:

- when speaking, in face-to-face social interaction, in simple transactions on the phone, and in group discussions, prepared debates, and presentations;
- when listening, in social interaction and using audio or video texts, including TV interviews and newscasts;
- when reading short literary texts, poems, and articles;
- when writing journals, letters, and essays.

TEXT TYPE

Students can:

- use simple discourse in a series of coherent paragraphs when speaking;
- understand most authentic spoken language when listening;
- create a series of coherent paragraphs when writing;
- acquire knowledge and new information from comprehensive, authentic texts when reading.

ACCURACY

Students:

- can engage in conversations with few significant patterns of error and use a wide range of appropriate vocabulary;
- demonstrate a heightened awareness of culturally appropriate behavior, although, as the task or message becomes more complex, they tend to become less accurate;
- are able to understand and report most key ideas and some supporting detail when reading and listening.

CONTENT

Content embraces:

- concepts of broader cultural significance, including institutions such as the education system, the government, and political and social issues in the target culture;
- topics of social and personal interest such as music, literature, the arts, and the sciences.

long you've known the person for whom you are writing, a detailed description of the individual's personal qualities, including a particular event that demonstrated one or more of the qualities you have described, and reasons why he/she will be a good counselor.

Please note that these student samples are not error free. They are reproduced here exactly as they were written. The original text was handwritten but is word processed here to facilitate reading. As you read each sample refer back to the appropriate stage performance expectations to determine why students received the score they did.

Cher Monsieur,

Je vous écrive cette lettre pour vous présenter mon ami, Jacques. Je crois que vous trouverez qu'il sera conseiller excellent. J'ai fait la connaissance d'Jacques il y a douze ans, a l'école maternelle. Même quand il était petit enfant, il etait gentil, amical, et tres agréable. Il soignait toujours ceux qui avaient besoin de son aide.

En plus, Jacques et intelligent et très amusant. Il peut être pensif, mais à la fois, il a l'esprit vif. Quand je suis triste, il me fait rire. Quand j'ai des problèmes, il m'écoute et il me comprend. C'est un bon ami.

Je peux vous assurez qu'Jacques sera un conseiller magnifique. Les enfants l'aiment toujours, surtout ceux de huit jusqu'a dix ans, à cause de son coeur léger. Chaque ete, il travaille comme conseiller, avec beaucoup de succès. Donc, il a beaucoup d'expérience avec les enfants et les camps d'ete.

Jacques est très responsable. Recemment, Jacques était chez moi. Mon petit frère, qui a neuf ans, s'est cassee le bras un escalant des arbres. Pendant que je le calmais et apaisais, Jacques téléphonait à ma mere, à Dr. Grandin, notre médecin, et à l'hôpital. Puis, il est rentré chez lui, et il est revenu en voiture pour apporter mon frère a l'hôpital. D'abord, Jacques restait avec nous pendant que nous attendions le medecin. Il nous a beaucoup aidé.

En somme, Jacques est amical, intelligent, responsable et sympathique - toutes les qualités qui sont nécessaire pour être bon conseiller. Si vous avez des questions, quoi qu'ils soient, n'hésitez pas de poser-les-moi.

Jeanne serait une conseilleure fantastique. Elle a l'experience avec les enfants parce qu'elle a un frère qui a di ans. Quand je vais chez elle, je peux voir Jeanne et son frere jouent au parc prèsque sa maison. Elle n'aime pas le football parce qu'elle pense que c'est trop violent mais toujours elle va au match de football de son frère. Après tous les matches elle le prend à la glacerie pour la glace chocolate. Elle est très genereuse je sais parce que quand je vais à la glacerie avec eux elle achète une glace pour moi.

Jeanne conduise lentement parce qu'elle a peur des accidents. Quand elle était jeune, son frère qui a 18 ans a un accident avec son voiture. Il etait tué. Jeanne pense que la famille c'est tres importante. Elle a beaucoup de sentiments pour sa famille. Ses parents ne sont pas stricte avec elle parceque ils savent qu'elle est responsable.

Quand Jeanne parle aux enfants, elle parle comme elle parle a une personne pas un gamin. Elle pense que tout le monde a besoin de respect. A la même fois, elle est la mère de tout le monde. Elle adore les enfants et ils l'adorent.

Jeanne est une excellente etudiante. Elle recoit le meillieur notes de sa classe. Elle veut ameilorer son education parce qu'elle eroit que les deux choses plus importantes son l'education et l'amour. Si un ami est triste elle l'aidera pas va a la classe. Elle veut apprendre l'histoire, l'analysis et la loi. Les artes l'interesse beaucoup. Toujours elle me prend au musee voir Toulouse Lautrec. Sa peinture favorite est Michalangelo et quand elle a lu "l'Agony et l'Ecstasy" elle pense que c'était le meuilleur biographie dans le monde. Maintenant après j'ai le lu je pense la même chose.

Jeanne est une personne terrifique et je pense que elle serait une conseilleur super!

Sinceremente,
XXXXXXXXXX

Chere mme Dupont,

Comment ca va? Ça va bien. Je vous écris parce que j'ai une amie qui voudrait travailler au camp en été. Elle s'appelle Mirielle et elle a dix-sept ans. Je la savais pour trois années et elle est ma meilleure amie. Elle adore les enfants et les enfants lui adore. Elle peut d'enseigner le tennis, le baseball, le basket, et le football parce qu'elle est très sportive. Elle joue aux sports en hiver, en été, en aton, et au printemps. Aussi, elle peut d'assister avec de la planche à voile, et elle peut de nager bien. Elle nage chez-elle, parce qu'elle a une piscine. Elle est une fille qui est très sympathique, par example, elle est toujours là quand quelqu'un a besoin de parler d'une probleme. Elle écoute bien et elle souvent répond avec les mots bons. Elle a une soeur qui a huit ans et elles s'entendent bien. Elle est très sympathique à sa soeur et elles se parlent beaucoup.

Finalement, elle a etudiée le français pour cinq cins, et elle parle bien. Si, vous acceptez Mirielle être une conseiller elle peut d'assister avec beaucoup de sports, elle peut de parler avec les enfants, et elle peut d'utiliser le français. Elle va être une bonne conseiller. Je vous promets.

STAGE V

Stage V is truly a very specialized stage in language development. Not all students will aspire to this stage, and it is a rare occurrence at the secondary level. However, with sufficient time, opportunity, and practice, nonnative speakers should be fully capable of realizing Stage V outcomes. It is well within the realm of possibility that a K-12 sequence may produce students who can perform consistently at this stage. Nevertheless, at the present time, it appears that few students through the sophomore year in college actually reach this stage.

The Stage V student is likely to be highly motivated and interested in pursuing further education and/or career opportunities where knowing a second or third language is a distinct advantage. Although some high school students with immersion experience may reach Stage V, the majority of Stage V learners are at the college and university level. The Stage V outcomes are included in the

LANGUAGE LEARNING CONTINUUM
STAGE V

FUNCTION

Students expand their ability to perform all the functions developed in Stages I, II, III, and IV. They also develop the ability to:

- conduct transactions and negotiations;
- substantiate and elaborate opinions;
- convince and persuade;
- analyze and critique.

CONTEXT

- Students can perform these functions in almost any context, including many complex situations.

TEXT TYPE

- Students can perform these functions in extended discourse when appropriate.

ACCURACY

Students:

- use culturally appropriate language, characterized by a wide range of vocabulary, with few patterns of error, although speech may contain some hesitation and normal pauses;
- comprehend significant ideas and most supporting details.

CONTENT

Content embraces:

- concepts of broader cultural significance, including social issues in the target culture, such as the environment and human rights;
- abstract ideas concerning art, literature, politics, and society.

Language Learning Continuum for the following reasons:

- Some students who are already beginning to function at Stage V need a challenge beyond the Stage IV outcomes.
- Although not all students will be able to achieve Stage V outcomes, they still need opportunities and practice at this level so that a strong foundation is provided for those who wish to move beyond Stage IV.
- College and university colleagues who teach world literature in the target language may find Stage V descriptions useful as a bridge between the Language Learning Continuum and the competencies necessary for the advanced study of literature. In the interest of a more coherent curriculum, dialogues between specialists in language acquisition and specialists in literature should continue.

Unlike the earlier stages, Stage V has no ceiling. The learning outcomes presume a wide focus that is not limited to literary content. Business and other professional endeavors, study abroad experiences, and a variety of graduate courses may all serve as points of departure for achieving Stage V outcomes.

In order to provide concrete examples of what Stage V performance "looks like," we have included below one sample in Spanish of written student work from each of the three categories used to describe student performance: (3) Exceeds Expectation, (2) Meets Expectation, and (1) Falls Below Expectation. (See full explanation on pp. 100-107.) Each of the samples falls within the parameters defined by Stage V for function, context, text type, accuracy, and content. The students whose work is shown here were given 40 minutes to consider what they were going to write, to write it, and to review and revise it, if necessary. The prompt was:

The Value of Friendship
Some people say that friendship is more important than money. Agree or disagree using examples from your own knowledge or experience.

Please note that these student samples are not error free. They are reproduced here exactly as they were written. The original text was handwritten but is word processed here to facilitate reading. As you read each sample refer back to the appropriate stage performance expectations to determine why students received the score they did.

SAMPLE 1 EXCEEDS EXPECTATION (SPANISH)

Algunas personas dicen que las amigos son más importantes que el dinero y yo estoy de acuerdo. Con dinero podemos tener muchas cosas materiales pero no tenemos nada emocional de importancia. Por ejemplo si yo tengo un problema yo puedo hablar con un de mis amigas porque ella entenderá lo que siento y me ayudará solver mi problema. Pero si no tengo ningunas amigas con que puedo hablar y confiarme en, quién vaya ayudarme? Vosotros todos necesitamos al menos un amigo con que podemos confiarnos en y divertirnos.

Aunque creo que en importante tener amigos, no creo que es necesito tener muchos. Yo mismo, tengo solamente un amigo con que yo puedo hablar de ciertas cosas y también tengo mi mejor amigo quien es mi novio. Le puedo decir todo a él. Como todos los amigos deben ser, el no es critico de mi y mi personaje. Esto, en mi opinion, es lo más importante entre amigos. Si no tienen esta confianza y si son critecos de cada uno, en realidad no son amigos. Los quienes son criticos de los otros solamente piensan siempre en su misma y el dinero. Con el dinero puedeu obtenes todo la que quieren para satisfacerse.

En mi opinion, y por mi expericiencia extensiva, los mejores amigos son los quienes su mayor importancia no es el dinero pero la buenventura de toda la gente. Por eso tengo solamente dos amigos en que puedo confiarme.

Creo que la amistad es más importante que el dinero. Tadavía hay la amistad, pero el dinero no dura por mucho tiempo. El dinero no puede comprarte ayuda, cómodo, amigos verdaderos, o algo que ura persona necesita para la salubridad mental. Si, dinero puede comprar cosas materiales, pero no va a ayudarte si es nuisero avaricioso, y miserable, porque ud estará solo. Si estará solo, dinero no tiene valor.

Mire a Donald Trump. El tenía mucho dinero, y parecía que tenía muchos amigos. Pero, cuando él perdió su dinero, tambien perdió sus amigos, y su esposa. Ésta muestra que la amistad tiene más valor que el dinero, porque él no tenia amigos verdaderos ellos solo le gusta para su dinero, y cuando su dinero salió tanbien salió sus amigos.

Mi tío tenia mucho dinero, y una familia loyal. Cuando el perdió su dinero, sus amigos y su familia lo ayuda. Aunque no tenía dinero, su familia lo todavía ayuda. La amistad de nuestra familia, y de sus amigos, tiene más valor que el dinero, porque el dinero salió, y su amistad dura.

Si tiene amigos que le gusta su dinero, no son amigos reales, porque ellos salarían cuando perdió su dinero. Pero, si tiere amigos reales y loyales, esta amistad dura cuando no tiene dinero. Ellos pueden ayudarle ganar más dinero para vivir. Esas cosas que las amistades dan es más importante que todo, incluye el dinero. Por eso, la amistad tiene mas valor que el dinero.

Yo creo que las amistades eran más importantes que el dinero. Mis amigas son aquí para mi siempre. Si yo necesite el consejo o simplemente alquien para decir con, yo se que mis amigos hacerían el tiempo. Cuando yo tenía un problema mis amigos son aqui para ayudarme siempre.

El dinero es differente. Con el dinero yo puedo comprar muchas cosas, pero nunca puedo compra alguna cosa que vale el que de la amistad. No puede comprar la amistad, y la amistad es la mas importante en la vida. Yo me encanta mis amigos. Yo sé que mis amigos eran aquí siempre para mi y saben que yo era aquí siempre para ellos. Yo espero que mis amistades viven para siempre.

Many more samples of student work that have not been evaluated can be found in Appendix F.

ficiency *Guidelines* contributed greatly to the cre-
Language Learning Continuum, but the two docu-
fferent. The ACTFL *Proficiency Guidelines* originated
th   em originally designed to assess the proficiency of U.S.
government personnel (Federal Interagency Language
Roundtable (FILR) Skill Level Definitions), whereas the
Language Learning Continuum was conceived from the outset for
use in a school environment, from grade 7 through the second
year of postsecondary education. Although both documents are
based on similar language components—function, content, context, text type, and accuracy—the Language Learning Continuum
contains additional information on suggested content appropriate
for classroom instruction at each stage.

How can the Language Learning Continuum guide interdisciplinary or project-based study?

By specifying both the content and functions appropriate to each
stage of language learning, the Language Learning Continuum
can help teachers select suitable areas and tasks for both projects
and interdisciplinary study at the appropriate level. For example,
Greek and Roman mythology is a common topic for study in
many middle schools.

Suggesting that Stage I students write short foreign language
versions of certain myths would be too difficult a task since narration is a Stage III function. However, providing information in
the content area of "family" is a Stage I function, and students
could create family trees that show the interrelationships among
mythological characters.

The student samples come from French and Spanish. How do the stages apply to German? Latin? Less commonly taught languages? ESL? Heritage learners?

Project participants included teachers of French, Spanish, and
Russian. In addition, samples were collected from German class-

rooms, where teachers reported on student outcomes that showed no significant differences from French or Spanish classrooms.

If ESL teachers begin to use the Language Learning Continuum, we believe that a good match is likely, but this possibility remains as yet untested. Where heritage learners have firsthand experiences with the target culture, they may need less practice in familiar content areas and exhibit more fluency and more accurate pronunciation, in addition to a heightened sense of cultural awareness. No information has been gathered on the Continuum's relationship to Latin and Greek.

What is the relationship between the Language Learning Continuum and the less able student?

Although using a performance-based curriculum with realistic assessments can lead to improved proficiency for all students, differences in student achievement will clearly be evident because students learn at varying rates. The Language Learning Continuum provides clear language for describing what students can do. Having an accurate description of student competence is the first step in communicating to students, their families, and other professionals. By using the Language Learning Continuum all interested parties can work collaboratively to meet individual students' needs by, for example, extending the time they are in a particular stage, or using specialized teaching techniques to address the students' learning styles.

The Language Learning Continuum was developed for use in grades 7-14. Does it have implications for grades K-6? 15-16?

The Language Learning Continuum can be helpful in describing both the proficiency of elementary school students as well as third- or fourth-year college/university students. Because the content of the first two stages is interchangeable, decisions related to introducing certain topics are not prescribed. Additionally, the content is similar to that of many elementary school curricula—family, community, professions. The sequence in which certain skills, such as reading and writing, are presented may differ in an elementary school language program where initial emphasis is placed on oral/aural language skills.

We expect continued progress through Stages III, IV, and possibly V from college students beyond the fourth semester of language study. Stages IV and V encompass many sophisticated skills and complex activities, and the Language Learning Continuum can provide reference points for instructors working at these higher levels in language, literature and culture.

How important is grammar in the context of the Language Learning Continuum? I don't see it mentioned.

Grammar contributes to the accuracy of language, and proficiency-based curricula often subsume grammar under the accuracy component of the Language Learning Continuum. In order to use and produce language accurately, a student needs to be knowledgeable about grammar, intonation, semantics, phonology, and cultural appropriateness. The Language Learning Continuum describes the level of accuracy expected at each of the five stages in relationship to the function, context, content, and text type encountered. The implication is clear: grammar is important, but it should not be the focus of second-language learning.

How long does it take to complete one stage?

As the Language Learning Continuum was originally conceived, it was suggested that each stage would equate approximately with two years of middle school study, one year of high school study, or one semester of college-level study. However, extensive field-testing in classrooms throughout New England indicated that student outcomes were very diverse, especially at Stage III, where few students attained Stage III proficiency by the end of their third year of high school language study or their third semester of college-level study. Many factors affect the length of time it takes students to complete any given stage, including the learner's age, interests, abilities, and exposure to native speakers or foreign travel; the instructor's abilities, interests, and methodology; and the program schedule, materials, and class sizes.

We are writing a new curriculum and we want to l it on the Language Learning Continuum. We also w to use portfolios. How should we start?

There is no one correct way to write a curriculum. Howeve effectively written curricula state clearly what students should know and be able to do, are research based, and are aligned with local, state, and national goals and/or standards.

First, determine the knowledge and skills that students will work to achieve. Refer to the appropriate stage description in the Language Learning Continuum and decide, based on past experience and samples of student work, which aspects of the function, context, text type, and accuracy descriptions students are expected to attain at each level.

Then, decide which combinations of topics to include. Refer to the content section of each stage description, along with national and state standards documents, school and department mission, philosophy and goal statements, and texts and other learning materials.

Next, decide what performance-based assessments will be used, as these assessments will determine the content of the teaching units, and the selection of items for the student portfolio.

As the final step, use each portfolio piece as a point of reference to develop the teaching units. Include grammatical structures, vocabulary, and planned classroom activities. Although this may be the extent of the public document, for internal use it may also prove helpful to develop a syllabus containing lists of materials, completion dates for assessments and assignments, and assessment rubrics.

I want my students to observe their own progress through the Language Learning Continuum. Can you recommend a way of doing this?

Provide students with a copy of the descriptions for all five stages of the Language Learning Continuum. After a brief introduction, direct them to underline or highlight the statements that describe what they can already do and the content areas in which they can do them. Next, highlight on an overhead transparency what the teacher expects them to know already and to achieve in the course of the year. As the year progresses, share the stage description again at the beginning and end of each unit, reminding students of the direction in which they are heading. In some advanced classes the teacher may want to discuss goals with the students, based on actual student work produced in past that clearly identifies accomplished skills, and discuss how best to meet the requirements of an advanced stage.

REFERENCES

Wiggins, Grant P. 1993. *Assessing Student Performance: Exploring the Purpose and Limits of Testing.* San Francisco, CA: Jossey-Bass, Inc.

CHAPTER 3

THE ISSUES OF CONTENT: LITERATURE AND CULTURE IN THE CONTINUUM

TEACHING CULTURE: A CONTRADICTION IN TERMS?

Language teachers have always struggled with the practical aspects of teaching culture. We are struck by the enormous complexity of cultural understanding and by the pedagogical contradictions implied when we join the words "teaching" and "culture" together. This is perhaps why, in the practical reality of the classroom, the cultural content of instruction has often been separated from the linguistic content and reduced to oversimplified "capsules" or mini-units. From the instructional perspective, understanding how to teach culture remains one of the most elusive goals of language instruction and one that deserves a great deal more attention in the professional domain. As important as what to teach and when to teach it, is the critical question of how to teach it.

The committees of teachers who drafted the *Standards for Foreign Language Learning* made a significant contribution to this effort when they defined the performance standards for cultural competence. The *Standards* state that students should "demonstrate an understanding of the relationship between the practices and the perspectives of the culture studied" (*Standards,* p. 46) and "of the relationship between the products and perspectives of the culture studied" (*Standards,* p. 47). The focus is on how people from different cultures *behave* and what people from different cultures *create*. In the Language Learning Continuum, *behavior* is implicit in the term "culturally appropriate," a term used to qualify accuracy of communication. The *creative* and *productive* aspect of the culture is embedded, however simply, in the content.

The discussion of exactly which literature, history, music, art, and current events to teach often yields a varied list of culturally appropriate practices that are successful in individual classrooms mainly because teachers have developed highly refined curriculum units on the topics, usually on their own with limited assistance and guidance from textbooks. This reality points to the need for utilizing new kinds of authentic materials that do not limit students in Stage I to menus and schedules, but invite learners to understand the culture of the language they are studying by being introduced to all aspects of it from the earliest possible point in study.

In this chapter, we open the discussion to the meaning and significance of culture and its role in the Language Learning Continuum. We share the ideas that have emerged from our ongoing discussion and debate about culture and literature in particular, about what it means when we say that students at various stages can interact productively with a broad spectrum of cultural artifacts, and how culture is embedded in the languages we teach.

TOWARD A DEFINITION OF CULTURE

Though no single, universally accepted definition of the word "culture" exists, there is general agreement that culture involves the ways of a people that distinguish them from other people. Culture is a system, based on patterned ways of perceiving and believing, of behaving and expressing, all in an integral and intertwined fashion. The products of a culture, such as clothing, artwork, and social institutions, reflect the operating mores of that culture. Underlying these products are components as complex as values and aesthetics. Furthermore, culture's dynamic nature, shaped by its evolution and geographic setting, affects people differently over time. Perhaps the very nature of this fluidity is at the root of the difficulty we experience in incorporating culture into the curriculum in a fully integrated fashion. If students are to discover the human connections and similarities we share with others as well as the diversity that makes each of us unique, they will need to develop the skills to understand the concept of culture, to analyze its components, and to interpret its meaning. If they are to acquire any degree of competence in understanding the complexities of culture, we, as teachers, must first understand it ourselves, and second, provide students with culturally authentic models that adapt the learner to the "text" (used here in the broader sense) and not the text to the learner.

CULTURE AND LANGUAGE

The integrated nature of the cultural content suggested by the *Standards* and by the Language Learning Continuum includes many components: literature, history, the arts, and current events. In practice, however, the culture component is often introduced separately, or, as is often the case in literature, is presented in glossed texts. If we expect students "to demonstrate an understanding of the interdependence and interaction of perspectives, products, and practices of a culture and its people," (*Standards*, p. 46) and, if the vehicle for deepening that understanding is through language acquisition, then instruction should be planned with an eye toward improving students' abilities to observe and analyze cultural phenomena. Thus, the heightening of cultural awareness becomes as important as language proficiency.

Proficiency in a language, including one's native language, is a key to acquiring cultural competence and to understanding that culture itself is a system of patterned behavior in which values are often culture dependent. In other words, culture is mediated through language and through the ways in which we think and talk about objects, events, and people, as well as imagine and even dream about them. A simple but clear example of how this works may be seen in the etymology of certain words.

The word *troubadour* in French or *trovador* in Spanish, for example, actually comes from an Arab word *tarabidour* meaning "the music-making that goes around," because the minstrels sang outdoors as they strolled about. *Flamenco* is also of Arab origin, derived from *ana fallah minkoum,* which means "I am a country person among you." Such etymological information underscores the fact that Moorish Spain between the eighth and fifteenth centuries was an unmatched cultural crossroads for Arab, North African, Jewish, and European traditions. The poetry and music that they nurtured formed the basis of much European culture, from classical music to troubadour style. These simple examples, readily available in every language, highlight the point that cultural ideas are intimately connected to what people say and to what they mean when they say it.

INTERPRETATION: A CRITICAL CULTURAL SKILL

How people choose to portray and present their culture is precisely what teachers can help convey to students as the underpinnings of the culture about which they are learning. Since culture is so closely tied to the way language is used, this means that culture is really dispersed across the four modalities—speaking, listening, reading, and writing—and is an integral part of thinking skills, or learning how to learn. If we believe that language skills are integrated with knowledge about a culture, then cultural knowledge should be placed as a high priority in instruction.

Here are some examples of how cross-cultural communication cuts across the four skill areas. Please note the importance of interpretation in these examples.

1. *Speaking,* or interpersonal communication, involves effective cross-cultural communication, that is, being able to size up the "speak" situation according to:

   a) participants, their age and gender

   b) the topic

   c) the register, that is, whether one is addressing a stranger, a close friend, a superior

   d) the physical situation, that is, where the conversation is taking place: on the street, in a school meeting, at a restaurant, or at work.

2. *Listening* is both interpersonal and interpretive and involves the same factors that apply to speaking. The ability to recognize the role of culture enters into play as does the recognition that culture provides ways to interpret meaning. When students understand that listening is more a question of interpretation than translation, they are not constantly filtering what they hear through their own system of assumptions; they are beginning to understand the importance of context.

3. *Reading* is a process that requires that students need to be able to interpret rather than translate. Granted, some kinds of reading, such as train schedules and some technical writing, are more literal across cultures, while others, such as literary texts, are highly interpretive. Some reading—

newspaper articles or expository prose for example—may be described as halfway between literal and interpretive.

4. *Writing* is also an interpersonal and an interpretive activity, whether the activity involves an exchange with a dialogue implied or is one-way and non-interactive, where no one is expected to respond. An example of interpersonal writing where interpretation and understanding of the culture is crucial is the formal written apology. In China, there are lists of acceptable apology formulas for every occasion. The Chinese often list things, but in American culture this is discouraged in favor of more descriptive narrative.

The reader-viewer-writer-listener, the student, is a maker of meaning who, in order to be successful while reading, listening and viewing, needs to interpret what he or she reads, hears, sees, and understands. In order to interpret, the student must have been given the tools to interpret as accurately as possible. The level of interpretational accuracy varies from learner to learner, but is closely interconnected with the stage of language development the learner has reached.

EDITING TASKS, NOT TEXTS

If one of the key factors in language proficiency and cultural competence is the student's stage of development, thoughtful choices must be made when planning all classroom activities. Lesson plans should be designed to draw from and enhance what students already know. The tasks that students are asked to carry out with specific content within a certain context may be organized to permit students to demonstrate a range of competence across one or more language-learning stages. These linguistic tasks, or "the things that get done with language" may range from asking and answering questions on familiar topics, to narrating and describing, to offering and defending an opinion, among others. The level of vocabulary may be concrete, relative or abstract, depending on the situation. Accuracy expectations will range from concept control to partial control to full control, while the text type they are encouraged to produce may be words and phrases, sentences or strings of sentences, a paragraph or extended discourse. In other words, authentic discourse is naturally uneven. Complex questions may elicit simple answers and vice-versa. For this reason, performance-based learning expectations such as the Language Learning Continuum are not meant to rigidly define the nature of student performance, but rather to encourage growth and to provide a context for measuring progress.

Keeping the above in mind as we implement instruction with the objective of teaching for cultural competence, it is clear that we need to substitute context-rich models for current generic models. Advances in technology such as interactive computer material, audio texts, videos, Web sites, and e-mail, to mention but a few, are now being harnessed by the publications industry to provide challenging opportunities for conveying reliable content-in-context about a culture and what its representatives say about it, as well as how they behave within its parameters. Knowing, for example, that today's students are accustomed to video texts and to the wealth of images they offer, we can fully appreciate the powerful tool that video offers for teaching and learning about culture. Verbal cues coupled with visual cues are doubly effective for conveying a variety of authentic messages on many different levels.

Multimedia resources that portray culture from within, in as unfiltered a fashion as possible, encourage us to acknowledge that culture actually means difference, or as Claire Kramsch has put it, "that culture is sometimes incommensurability of viewpoints, of world view" (University of New Hampshire Workshop, 1993). By exploring the language-in-context of target cultures through a variety of texts, we can increase opportunities for students to understand that there is always something going on "underneath" words, behavior, and images that may, at first, seem not to make sense. Speculation and hypothesis over what is really going on require patience and a willingness to suspend judgment so that the easy reactions that "it is just stupid" or "they don't do it like we do" do not hold sway.

For the average student, thinking and learning about culture often takes place in what Vicki Galloway has referred to as a kind of "neutralized tourist zone," (Pennsylvania State University Workshop, 1987). This "N.T.Z." is devoid of ambiguities and tolerates absurd behavior by the tourist. As a student's cultural competence grows, there is gradual movement out of this "zone" as contact increases in more varied contexts within the target environment.

IMPLICATIONS FOR INSTRUCTION

From the instructional perspective, it is important for teachers to provide students with specific goals that focus on cultural conventions, connotations, and conditions in their corresponding contexts. Teaching about culture should follow an organizational schema rather than random information or piecemeal knowledge that provides only a partial or a distorted view. In this way, we can provide a more favorable environment for cultural proficiency to develop on a par with oral proficiency. Any degree of success in teaching cultural competence will depend in great part on recognition of the fact that we cannot really speak accurately and knowledgeably about culture without a context, nor can we speak about language without culture. For this reason, the Language Learning Continuum suggests that the focus of Stages I and II be the core content represented by the common vocabulary that we all use to communicate on a daily basis. Stage III can focus on *important people* and their contributions. Stage IV should expand to include *culturally significant institutions*, and Stage V should reach into the domain of *issues*. By establishing this relatively simple and flexible framework, teachers can choose topics that are both relevant and manageable from the learner's perspective.

The neglect of cultural realities has serious consequences. This is especially evident when students have to interact with real people for whom they have no authentic cultural context, whom they cannot understand or appreciate, and with whom they cannot communicate. Keep in mind that a foreign language is not simply a difficult way to speak English, nor are different patterns of behavior around the world simply deviations from a set of norms derived from one's own culture.

CULTURAL CONCEPTS THROUGH THE STAGES

The Language Learning Continuum does not limit or define the cultural components of a language program. It is the belief of the teachers who developed the Continuum that the teaching of literature and culture is unlimited by nature and that students are able to enter the target culture at any stage, whether that entry is characterized by an activity as simple as word identification (a possible Stage I activity), classroom discussion (a typical Stage II or III activity), or as complex as literary analysis (a typical Stage IV activity).

As we incorporate the cultural component into the content of any given stage, creative teaching emerges. Mindful of the five components that make up each stage—content, context, function, text type, and accuracy—we can create lessons and assessments that provide students access to the text (literary, historical, video, art) commensurate with their progress. The challenge of presenting authentic cultural content will reap its own rewards in the knowledge our students will gain about the target culture and how they apply that knowledge to their understanding of themselves and the world at large. The examples provided below for Spanish and Chinese instruction suggest ways to incorporate important cultural concepts throughout the Language Learning Continuum.

ACTIVITIES WITH A CULTURAL FOCUS FOR THE SPANISH LANGUAGE CLASSROOM

THE CONCEPT OF DEATH IN MEXICO'S *DÍAS DE LOS MUERTOS*

The annual *días de los muertos* that are widely celebrated in Mexico at the end of October and early November provide a wealth of insight into the ways in which people of all ages think about death, face it, and represent it in various and interesting guises in their culture. The fact that the Spanish concepts and manifestations of death have their origin in pre-Hispanic worldviews that were combined with European Roman Catholic traditions dating back to the seventh century, has created a rich cultural fusion that is very much alive among people of all social classes in Mexico today. The universal questions of who we are, how we came to be, and where we will go are portrayed and at least partially answered in a myriad colorful, imaginative, and playful ways.

This multifaceted cultural topic, accompanied by appropriate activities, lends itself well to the learning of process skills and their immediate application in Spanish and encourages the use of the language on concrete, relative, and abstract levels. It promotes collaborative or cooperative work and increases students' awareness of the richness and diversity of other cultures beyond their own, helping them to be attuned to similarities and differences worth knowing, and even celebrating.

Working in groups of three or four, students at all stages (I-V) can be assigned content areas to be explored in stage-appropriate fashion, using Spanish to acquire their information. In Stages I and II, access to this information might be provided by brief articles, photo collections, videos, and posters. At Stages III and IV, sources would include more sophisticated articles as well as literary texts (stories, poems, novels). Students would be asked to research processions, special Masses, the cleaning of tombstones, all-night vigils in the graveyard, the making of flowered pathways, the construction of special altars, a variety of offerings, and the welcoming and farewell of souls returning to earth. Other topics that suggest themselves are the symbolic value of: sugar skulls, incense, candles, flowers of the dead, papier mâché skeletons, bread of the dead, death portraits of the living in verse, death motifs on decorative cut-out tissue paper, and special food. Each of these activities leads, in a variety of ways, to an understanding of the way in which the people of Mexico traditionally choose to deal with matters of life and death. Keeping the Language Learning Continuum in mind, a few examples of activities appropriate for each stage follow.

STAGE I ACTIVITIES FOR *EL DÍA DE LOS MUERTOS*

The teacher provides a general introduction that includes the vocabulary to be learned for asking and answering the right questions on the topic in general and the subtopics in particular. Stress is placed on the importance of integrating all four language skills into the process. Students make a series of vocabulary cards with illustrations or create poster collages with labeled items, including nouns as well as accompanying adjectives. These visual products may be used for prompts for brief show-and-tell presentations to the rest of the class at the word and simple sentence level. Another possibility is to hold up photos or drawings without labeled vocabulary to elicit responses in which students identify what the visuals depict.

STAGE II ACTIVITIES FOR *EL DÍA DE LOS MUERTOS*

While content is similar to that of Stage I, at Stage II students are more proficient. They are able to provide more detail, to use strings of sentences, to practice simple descriptions of what the photos and drawings depict on a concrete level. The focus can shift from objects to what people are doing. Projects may include constructing a decorated altar with its accompanying offering, making papier mâché skeletons, preparing bread of the dead from a recipe, and putting together an album of photographs with accompanying descriptions.

STAGE III ACTIVITIES FOR *EL DÍA DE LOS MUERTOS*

Stage III requires increasingly greater concentration on narration and description. Venturing into the complex realm of offering and supporting an opinion may also be appropriate—preparing the student for the more sophisticated functions that characterize Stages IV and V. One useful activity is to interview native speakers from Mexico. The interview could be videotaped or recorded and summarized by students. In addition, oral reports of varying lengths might be required of the students, to include descriptions, narration (i.e., what occurs on the first, second, and third days of the celebration), as well as contrasting and comparing *El Día de los Muertos* traditions in Mexico with those of other cultures, such as Halloween in the United States. The report might be in written form as well, and subjected to peer review prior to final submission.

STAGES IV AND V ACTIVITIES FOR *EL DÍA DE LOS MUERTOS*

Thematically pertinent short stories, novels, and discussion groups are a rich resource for activities requiring descriptive as well as analytical skills. A debating panel works well to elicit not only descriptions, but also opinions on more abstract levels relating to spirituality, attitudes toward death, cultural conditioning, and contrasts in belief systems. Critical essays and research papers might emerge from the above activities with a focus on performing the advanced functions associated with these last two stages in the Language Learning Continuum.

Activities with a Cultural Focus for the Chinese Language Classroom

Activities submitted by Yu-Lan Lin, Boston Public Schools

The Celebration of the Chinese New Year
Stage I Activities

The objectives for this activity are for students to identify objects used for the New Year and to observe how Chinese people interact during the New Year celebration. Since the Chinese New Year celebration starts with people decorating their homes, a teacher can start this celebration by decorating the classroom in the following way.

Step One: Set up a "shrine" on a bookshelf or a small table. On the shrine, there should be some fruit, such as oranges and tangerines, as well as sweet pastries, nuts, and candies for good luck.

Step Two: Decorate the classroom with red, pink, or New Year's flowers, such as narcissus.

Step Three: Write words like *fu* (blessing) or *chun* (spring) on large pieces of red paper to be displayed on classroom doors.

Step Four: Prepare red envelopes containing a lucky penny for each student. The teacher first introduces the customs of preparing for the New Year, then explains the symbolic meanings of displayed objects. Second, the teacher introduces New Year phrases, such as *xing nian kuai le* (Happy New Year) or *gong xi fa cai* (Wishing you a prosperous year). Finally the teacher has the students role-play the customary exchange of *hong bao* (red envelopes).

The objectives for this activity are for students to further examine the symbolic meanings of New Year related objects and to convert the Gregorian calendar year into the animal zodiac year. For this activity the teacher decorates the room with more red scrolls of *chun lian* (spring couplets) like, "May your studies continue to be successful," or "May your land continue to be productive." On the shrine, a tray of eight compartments, each containing dried fruit, seeds, nuts, sweets, and candies, can be added. On the board, a large 12-animal zodiac with the corresponding Gregorian year written under each animal is posted.

The teacher explains the literal meaning of each *chun lian* and the symbolic meaning of the eight kinds of food displayed in the tray. The class then plays a guessing game utilizing these objects. For the animal zodiac activity, the teacher explains the origin of the 12-animal zodiac. Next, the students learn the names of the 12 animals, and learn to convert the Gregorian year to the zodiac year by using the display. Each student will identify his or her zodiac animal and also be able to convert any given year into the proper animal zodiac year.

The objective for this activity is for students to understand the Chinese practice of ancestor and deity worship on New Year's Day. More celebratory New Year food offerings such as *nian gao* (New Year rice cake) and *jiao zi* (Peking ravioli) may be added to the shrine. Pictures of different deities (kitchen god, earth god, fire god, door god) and "ancestors" can be displayed on the wall as well. "Firecrackers" of red construction paper and paper lanterns can be made by students to decorate the entrance of the classroom. The teacher tells traditional stories of the deities, such as the one explaining how people prepare the sticky rice cake to sweeten and seal the mouth of the kitchen god. After the story, the students sample the *nian gao*.

The teacher discusses the practice of food offerings by introducing some important traditional family concepts understood by the Chinese people through the teachings of Confucius. The students taste *jiao zi* and other food offerings afterward. Finally, the students will role play the practice of *bai nian* (visiting friends on New Year's Day) using culturally appropriate verbal and nonverbal behavior.

The objectives for this activity are for students to compare the traditional Chinese family structure and the new structure under the current Chinese policy, and make an assessment of its impact on the New Year celebration and on the overall welfare of China.

The teacher first shows video clips such as *xiao xi* ("Little Happiness") or takes a descriptive section from different books depicting traditional Chinese families and/or contemporary Chinese families. After this initial introduction through the literary texts and tapes, the students are ready to discuss how the New Year celebration has changed from the way it was in the past, by traditional extended families, to the way it is now, by current one-child families. Students are encouraged to hold a debate on the pros and cons of these two family structures and their impact on the welfare of the country in the future.

The objectives for this activity are for students to compare three schools of philosophy and to analyze what influences each one has had on the celebration of the New Year.

The teacher first introduces sections from *lun yu* (Confucius' *Analects*), teachings and writings from Lao Zi and Zhuang Zi, as well as Buddhist concepts of life and family. Next, the teacher will guide the students to conduct individual research on what influences these schools of thought had on topics such as ancestor worship, deity worship, ethics, and conduct. Students can make oral presentations based on their research, comparing and contrasting the most important aspects of each philosophy.

THE CULTURE OF LITERATURE

The preceding examples of Spanish and Chinese learning activities highlight instructional strategies for teaching certain customs and beliefs pertinent to the target culture. The study of great literature is another powerful means for helping students better understand the culture and develop the skills and insight needed to integrate their learning. From the earliest stages of language study, students can begin to acquire the skills needed to learn about culture through the stimulating content of important works of literature. As students begin to recognize universal themes presented in literature, they begin to connect and empathize with other human beings. Montaigne's sixteenth-century essay on education addresses many of the same issues that our schools face today just as Rimbaud's nineteenth-century poetry speaks to the creative genius and rebellious nature of every young generation. Haven't we all thought of ourselves occasionally as "tilting at windmills?" Literature helps students understand and dignify the concerns, values, and feelings held in common by all people.

Literature also defines our differences. Each literary tradition provides a small but significant window into the distinctive culture of its creator. Students learn to appreciate the uniqueness of each culture, gaining information about the differences between its social institutions, customs, beliefs, and attitudes and their own. Through literature, students learn about what others have written, believed, and said; they gain access to a range of human ideas and human values, thus broadening their own perspective. Since literature serves as a record of others' behaviors and reactions to the surrounding world, a study of literature can help students develop criteria to evaluate their own responses to the world. In addition, a broad literary exposure encourages students to be more flexible in their thinking, contributes positively to students' communicative competence, and refines their reading, writing, analytical, and expressive skills. Finally, literature offers an opportunity to connect with other disciplines. Historical contexts, scientific inventions and discoveries, comparative genres, and artistic interpretations can all be explored and experienced.

LITERATURE FOR ALL STAGES

Our task as teachers is to provide literary materials rich in cultural patterns and a framework enabling students to discover these patterns for themselves. Stimulating content does not have to be saved until mastery of linguistic skills has been attained. Even in Stage I, students can be exposed to and become familiar with literature. It is possible to allude briefly, yet frequently, to well-known works of art and literature without complex discussion. Foreign terms and phrases, short maxims and proverbs, and even quotes may serve to prepare students for the frequency of literary allusions in the media and in conversation. The film version of a play—subtitles and all—introduces students to a creative outlet that will carry deeper significance as they acquire greater expertise in interpreting meaning. At Stages II and III, any allusion to a literary work may be an opportunity to introduce other cultural components, including the history, music, and government of the age in which it was written. Literary allusions serve as an entry point for a wider exposition of cultural life.

Teaching poetry and excerpts at Stage III and longer literary texts at Stages IV and V further expands the student's understanding of the cultural milieu in which the work was written. A matrix of the author's life, the choice of vocabulary that carries cultural significance, the society's values, and the arts that embrace the literary work contribute to the repertoire of this approach. The authors of "Building Multiple Proficiencies in New Curriculum Contexts" define literacy as "the activity by which we define ourselves and make meaning of phenomena and human experience in general" (Jurasek and Jurasek, p. 92). As "outsiders" looking in, observing, judging, and comparing the target culture to their own, students incorporate a multitude of perspectives into the learning experience leading to literacy. Even if our students never live in the target culture and if only a few ever use their skills as tourists, they will, nevertheless, benefit from a focus on literacy leading to cultural competency.

The sample activities that follow, while certainly not exhaustive, exemplify "editing the task, not the text." The examples used and the processes described can be easily replicated using major works of literature from any period or culture.

MINGLING REALITY WITH ILLUSION: THE POETRY OF JACQUES PRÉVERT

Jacques Prévert, born in 1900, was particularly successful as a writer of film scripts. After World War II, however, he steadily gained popularity and renown as a poet. Many of his poems satirize the manners and politics of his society, but in others, Prévert enchants us with his fantasies mingling reality and illusion. Introducing the following poems through the stages provides another demonstration of tailoring the task while not changing the text. From the earliest stages, students may begin the process of comprehensive reading, which will include an initial understanding, an interpretation of meaning, making connections to personal and world schemata, and a critical stance. Prévert's poetry is easily accessed, has nearly universal appeal, and offers cultural insight often combined with refreshing and youthful humor.

STAGE I—"REFRAINS ENFANTINS"

In introducing the concept of masculine and feminine gender, we want to differentiate between sociolinguistic and grammatical structures and purposes. In his poem, "Refrains enfantins," Prévert reprimands us, through a child's perspective, for using the masculine pronoun in most common idiomatic expressions. Stage I learners can make valuable use of this poem as they move away from the concept of neuter gender. A similar dilemma would not exist in the English language. This easily memorized poem can be set to music.

Refrains enfantins

Il pleut Il pleut
  Il fait beau
Il fait du soleil
  Il est tôt
Il se fait tard
    Il
    Il
    Il
    Il
  Toujours Il
Toujours Il qui pleut et qui neige
  Toujours Il qui fait du soleil
    Toujours Il
  Pourquoi pas Elle
    Jamais Elle
  Pourtant Elle aussi
  Souvent se fait belle.

(From *Spectacle*, © Éditions GALLIMARD.)

STAGE II—"PAGE D'ÉCRITURE"

The world of the Stage II learner is usually entrenched in the educational environment, which connects easily to the target culture, as students learn about differences and similarities of attitudes. Prévert has written several poems on the theme of education, including "Page d'écriture," which portrays the student dreamer in the rigid environment of a classroom. Stage II learners are able to identify many of the vocabulary words they have studied in this poem. The French classroom described may present more of an historical image than the present reality, but the contrasts are important and interesting.

Reading for interpretation allows Stage II learners to visualize the classroom ambiance through the eyes of the young narrator. Describing and comparing the child's situation to their own as students in school, Stage II learners begin to express individual emotions as they make connections.

Page d'écriture

Deux et deux quatre

quatre et quatre huit

huit et huit font seize

Répétez! dit le maître

Deux et deux quatre

quatre et quatre huit

huit et huit font seize

Mais voilà l'oiseau-lyre

qui passe dans le ciel

l'enfant le voit

l'enfant l'entend

l'enfant l'appelle

Sauve-moi

joue avec moi

oiseau!

Alors l'oiseau descend

et joue avec l'enfant

Deux et deux quatre…

Répétez! dit le maître

et l'enfant joue

l'oiseau joue avec lui…

Quatre et quatre huit

huit et huit font seize

et seize et seize qu'est-ce qu'ils font?

Ils ne font rien seize et seize

et surtout pas trente-deux

de toute façon

et ils s'en vont.

Et l'enfant a caché l'oiseau

dans son pupitre

et tous les enfants

entendent sa chanson

et tous les enfants

entendent la musique

et huit et huit à leur tour s'en vont

et quatre et quatre et deux et deux

à leur tour fichent le camp

et un et un ne font ni une ni deux

un et un s'en vont également.

Et l'oiseau-lyre joue

et l'enfant chante

et le professeur crie:

Quand vous aurez fini de faire le pitre!

Mais tous les autres enfants

écoutent la musique

et les murs de la classe

s'écroulent tranquillement.

Et les vitres redeviennent sable

l'encre redevient eau

les pupitres redeviennent arbres

la craie redevient falaise

la porte-plume redevient oiseau.

(From *Paroles*, © Éditions GALLIMARD.)

Stage III—"Déjeuner du matin"

The well-known poem, "Déjeuner du matin," leaves more to interpretation than one may realize after an initial reading. Who is speaking in the poem? A married woman? Or could it be a child, a friend, or a parent? What is the relationship of this person with the "other" described? We know Stage III learners to be inquisitive and curious. The open interpretation of such a poem allows the learner to stretch his or her imagination and frame it in the target language. The cultural setting of the poem is remarkable in its simplicity. Like the Japanese tea ceremony, this scene is replete with symbolism related to the breakfast "ceremony." Students may describe their morning eating rituals or those of people they observe.

This poem has often been introduced when teaching the *passé composé* in French. What is the significance of this past-tense form throughout the poem? Is the poet describing a habitual activity or a moment in time? In what sense is this poetry?

Déjeuner du matin

Il a mis le café

Dans la tasse

Il a mis le lait

Dans la tasse de café

Il a mis le sucre

Dans la tasse de café

Avec la petite cuiller

Il a tourné

Il a bu le café au lait

Et il a reposé la tasse

Sans me parler

Il a allumé

Une cigarette

Il a fait des ronds

Avec la fumée

Il a mis les cendres

Dans le cendrier

Sans me parler

Sans me regarder

Il s'est levé

Il a mis

Son chapeau sur sa tête

Il a mis

Son manteau de pluie

Parce qu'il pleuvait

Et il est parti

Sous la pluie

Sans une parole

Sans me regarder

Et moi j'ai pris

Ma tête dans ma main

Et j'ai pleuré.

(From *Paroles*, © Éditions GALLIMARD.)

STAGE IV—"POUR FAIRE LE PORTRAIT D'UN OISEAU"

Fairy tales and illusion techniques such as those manifested in director Jean Cocteau's film *La Belle et La Bête* allow students to explore the unknown through stories they remember from childhood. In similar fashion, in Prévert's world of fantasy, animate and inanimate objects combine whimsically. One fine example that works very well with students is his wonderful poem "Pour faire le portrait d'un oiseau." Using this poem provides an extraordinary tool for asking questions such as "What is freedom?" Such questions are enjoyed by students at this stage as they develop their ability to begin to explain and support their opinions.

Pour faire le portrait d'un oiseau

Peindre d'abord une cage

avec une porte ouverte

peindre ensuite

quelque chose de joli

quelque chose de simple

quelque chose de beau

quelque chose d'utile

pour l'oiseau

placer ensuite la toile contre un arbre

dans un jardin

dans un bois

ou dans une forêt

se cacher derrière l'arbre

sans rien dire

sans bouger…

Parfois l'oiseau arrive vite

mais il peut aussi bien mettre de longues années

avant de se décider

ne pas se décourager

attendre

attendre s'il le faut pendant des années

la vitesse ou la lenteur de l'arrivée de l'oiseau

n'ayant aucun rapport

avec la réussite du tableau

Quand l'oiseau arrive

s'il arrive

observer le plus profond silence

attendre que l'oiseau entre dans la cage

et quand il est entré

fermer doucement la porte avec le pinceau

puis

effacer un à un tous les barreaux

en ayant soin de ne toucher aucune des plumes de

l'oiseau

Faire ensuite le portrait de l'arbre

en choississant la plus belle de ses branches

pour l'oiseau

peindre aussi le vert feuillage et la fraîcheur du vent

la poussière du soleil

et le bruit des bêtes de l'herbe dans la chaleur de l'été

et puis attendre que l'oiseau se décide à chanter

Si l'oiseau ne chante pas

c'est mauvais signe

signe que le tableau est mauvais

mais s'il chante c'est bon signe

signe que vous pouvez signer

Alors vous arrachez tout doucement

une des plumes de l'oiseau

et vous écrivez votre nom dans un coin du tableau.

(From *Paroles*, © Éditions GALLIMARD.)

STAGE V—"BARBARA"

When students have achieved a near-native level of language proficiency, the content of their instruction may include concepts of broader cultural significance. Prévert's "Barbara" introduces the subject of war and peace; the juxtaposition of a tender moment in time remembered amidst the horror of destruction. Using this work students can develop and craft their skills of analysis and critique as they learn of an experience that may not be one they can relate to personally. The historical underpinnings of the poet's message are ready to be explored and discussed. Debates, critical essays, and extensive research are all possible at this stage.

Barbara

Rappelle-toi Barbara

Il pleuvait sans cesse sur Brest ce jour-là

Et tu marchais souriante

Épanouie ravie ruisselante

Sous la pluie

Rappelle-toi Barbara

Il pleuvait sans cesse sur Brest

Et je t'ai croisée rue de Siam

Tu souriais

Et moi je souriais de même

Rappelle-toi Barbara

Toi que je ne connaissais pas

Toi qui ne me connaissais pas

Rappelle-toi

Rappelle-toi quand même ce jour-là

N'oublie pas

Un homme sous un porche s'abritait

Et il a crié ton nom

Barbara

Et tu as couru vers lui sous la pluie

Ruisselante ravie épanouie

Et tu t'es jetée dans ses bras

Rappelle-toi cela Barbara

Et ne m'en veux pas si je te tutoie

Je dis tu à tous ceux que j'aime

Même si je ne les ai vus qu'une seule fois

Je dis tu à tous ceux qui s'aiment

Dont il ne reste rien

Même si je ne les connais pas

Rappelle-toi Barbara

N'oublie pas

Cette pluie sage et heureuse

Sur ton visage heureux

Sur cette ville heureuse

Cette pluie sur la mer

Sur l'arsenal

Sur le bateau d'Ouessant

Oh Barbara

Quelle connerie la guerre

Qu'es-tu devenue maintenant

Sous cette pluie de fer

De feu d'acier de sang

Et celui qui te serait dans ses bras

Amoureusement

Est-il mort disparu ou bien encore vivant

Oh Barbara

Il pleut sans cesse sur Brest

Comme il pleuvait avant

Mais ce n'est plus pareil et tout est abîmé

C'est une pluie de deuil terrible et désolée

Ce n'est même plus l'orage

De fer d'acier de sang

Tout simplement des nuages

Qui crèvent comme des chiens

Des chiens qui disparaissent

Au fil de l'eau sur Brest

Et vont pourrir au loin

Au loin très loin de Brest

Dont il ne reste rien.

(From Paroles, © Éditions GALLIMARD.)

ART FOR ALL STAGES

Submitted by Margaret Langford, Keene State College

Without thinking too much about it, we often say that a picture is worth a thousand words. We all know the evocative power of France's "liberté, égalité, fraternité." We associate this rallying cry of the French Revolution with many Francophone practices and products. Linking the motto first with two specific works of art, we will show how Delacroix's *Liberty Guiding the People* and Rousseau's *The Representatives of Foreign Powers Coming to Salute the Republic as a Sign of Peace* can serve as focal points for cultural activities from Stages I through V.

These two paintings, well known and easily accessible to all teachers, offer many possibilities for speaking, listening, and writing activities that connect with personal and historic pasts and provide the opportunity for teaching culture in context. Both reveal Liberty in a crowded square where people of all ages are enacting an important event.

In Delacroix's painting, a lightly clad Liberty strides forward out of a dark and ominous background filled with gun smoke. Tricolor in hand, she looks to her right, seemingly encouraging the armed men and boys pressing forward toward the unseen

enemy. We can see that the fight has already taken its toll. A gentleman in a top hat who's armed with a rifle and a pistol-waving street urchin accompany Liberty as the crowd surges forward over the bodies of dead comrades. The blue, white, and red of the tricolor in Liberty's hand and the descending light surrounding her, briefly touching the street urchin and the soldiers, contrast strikingly with the darkened square, gun smoke, and somber clothing of the throng of men and boys.

In contrast, Rousseau's Liberty, swathed in red, holds out an olive branch to the heads of nations standing stiffly at attention under a canopy. The square is peaceful. On the right we see buildings festooned with banners, children dancing sedately around a statue. There are no signs of violence—no gun smoke, no somber masses. A few white clouds appear here and there in an otherwise clear blue sky. The red, white, and blue of the tricolor is repeated in the flags waving on top of the canopy, in the dignitaries' sashes and uniforms, and in the boys' trousers. There is color everywhere. In the foreground, gold writing on urns filled with olive branches proclaims: "peace, work, liberty, fraternity."

The following activities suggest strategies that permit and encourage students at every stage of the Language Learning Continuum to study the works of important artists as part of their language instruction.

STAGE I WRITING ACTIVITY

You are observing this scene from the balcony of your hotel. Write a postcard to a friend including at least three of the following:

1) today's date and the time you are writing your card
2) what the weather is like today
3) a description of someone or something you see
4) a description of what one or more of the people are doing

Add anything else you feel would make your postcard interesting and complete.

STAGE I GROUP PERFORMANCE ACTIVITY

"Eyewitness News." Choose one of the paintings and present a broadcast as if you were witnessing the scene live. Possible roles include sign maker, weatherperson, background expert, interviewer, etc.

STAGE II WRITING ACTIVITY

You are visiting France. From your hotel room balcony, you witness the scene in the painting before you. Describe what you see as fully as possible. State which is your favorite concept of the three in the motto "liberté, égalité, fraternité" and why.

STAGE II GROUP PERFORMANCE ACTIVITY

We can transform the Stage I "Eyewitness News" into a Stage II activity by taking Stage II function, text type, and context into account. For example, besides stating the date, time, and place of the event, the announcer might provide more detailed program highlights.

The learners emerging into Stage III are making a quantum language leap. They are inquisitive, inventive, and eager to be independent. As in the previous stages, students will do background preparation prior to working on their performance pieces. At this stage, an individualized student portfolio of reading, listening, and/or viewing selections can work quite well. From a list provided by the instructor, students will choose their own selections and look for information that will be relevant to the "Eyewitness News" broadcast. This activity can be recast as a roundtable discussion or a talk-show interview with one or more interview subjects.

You are an Acadian visiting France. You are writing to a cousin whose branch family settled in Fort Kent, Maine, following the dispersal of Acadians from Canada. Looking from your hotel window, you witness the events depicted in the picture. Incorporating as much detail as possible, tell your cousin what has happened up to this point and how the events make you feel. Remember that as an Acadian you are particularly impassioned by the concepts of liberté, égalité, and fraternité.

At Stage IV we find risk-takers who monitor their language production and who self-correct. Stage IV learners can perform a wide variety of tasks. They can listen to and understand news broadcasts, view films without subtitles, easily engage in conversations with French speakers, and read a wide variety of printed texts.

Increasingly independent learners, Stage IV students respond well to individualized learning portfolios, which allow choices in background reading and viewing materials. Access to the Internet and to French language newscasts and television may or may not be available to students in all schools.

However, many families have access to one or all. Portfolio preparation could include information gathered from these sources. Some additional sources to be placed on their reading list might include: *Les droits de l'homme*, Tocqueville's *De L'Amérique*, Balzac's *Le Colonel Chabert*, Hugo's *Les Misérables*, Zola's *Germinal*, the works of Gabrielle Roy, or Miriama Bâ's *Une si longue lettre*. A performance activity at this stage may take the form of a panel discussion or debate.

STAGE IV WRITING ACTIVITY

You are an older version of one of the figures in the painting you see before you. Ten years have passed since you participated in this event. Taking into account what you were like then and what you are like now, explain how this event transformed your life.

STAGE V ACTIVITIES

Stage V learners are highly motivated. Often they consider French an integral part of their advanced educational and/or career plans. They welcome challenges and perform adequately in almost any context. Since the Stage V learner is so versatile, one way of changing the performance activity at this stage is to change the composition of the participants and audience members. In other words, one can include "real" French speakers: graduates who have spent time abroad, exchange students, and members of the community.

Written activities might include authentic tasks such as writing to the French language Internet conversation group about these two works of art, or debating which of the works best represents the concepts of liberté, égalité, and fraternité. Students may be asked to state their case and defend their point of view. Delacroix's painting, Rousseau's, or others of equally rich potential can serve as cultural foci for performance and writing activities spiraled through the stages.

FREQUENTLY ASKED QUESTION

I notice that the Language Learning Continuum makes continued reference to improved reading ability throughout the five stages. Hasn't reading been de-emphasized in recent years due to the focus on oral communicative skills?

Reading continues to be an integral part of second language learning, and two standards taken as examples from the national Standards for Language Learning provide clear reasons for the important role of reading: "Students reinforce and further their knowledge of other disciplines through the foreign language" (Standard 3.1) and "Students acquire information and recognize the distinctive viewpoints that are available only through the foreign language and its cultures" (Standard 3.2). In today's computer-assisted information age, the knowledge stored in the world's greatest libraries and databases is immediately accessible to those who can read the language in which they are written. Developing reading skills in our students is vital so that as adults they can understand whole bodies of information—newspapers, books, journal reports—that would otherwise be incomprehensible to them. Reading is also the principal key to unique cultural understandings offered by literature in the target language. Using instructional methods that emphasize "editing the task, not the text" encourages even the youngest learners to begin to develop more sophisticated understanding of the target culture through reading.

REFERENCES

Bacon, Susan M. 1995. "Coming to Grips with the Culture: Another Use of Dialogue Journals in Teacher Education." *Foreign Language Annals* 28 (summer).

Byrnes, Heidi, ed. 1992. *Languages for a Multicultural World in Transition*. Lincolnwood, IL: National Textbook Company.

Goodenough, Ward. 1981. *Culture, Language and Society*. Menlo Park, CA: Cummings.

Hall, Edward T. 1976. *Beyond Culture*. New York: Doubleday.

Jurasek, Barbara S. and Richard T. Jurasek. 1991. "Building Multiple Proficiencies in New Curriculum Contexts." In *Building Bridges and Making Collaborations*, edited by

June K. Phillips. Middlebury, VT: Northeast Conference on the Teaching of Foreign Languages.

Kramsch, Claire J. 1993. *Context and Culture in Language Teaching*. New York: Oxford University Press.

Lado, Robert. 1957. *Linguistics Across Cultures: Applied Linguistics for Language Teachers*. Ann Arbor: University of Michigan Press.

Lafayette, Robert C., ed. 1996. *National Standards: A Catalyst for Reform*. Lincolnwood, IL: National Textbook Co. (ACTFL Language Education Series).

National Standards in Foreign Language Education Project. 1996. *Standards for Foreign Language Learning: Preparing for the 21st Century*. Yonkers, NY: The National Standards in Foreign Language Education Project.

O'Malley, J. Michael and Anna Uhl Chamot. 1990. *Learning Strategies in Second Language Acquisition*. Cambridge: Cambridge University Press.

Rissel, Dorothy. Spring 1995. "Learning by Doing: Outcomes of an Overseas Summer Project for Teachers." *Foreign Language Annals* 28 (spring).

Stevick, Earl. 1998. *Teaching and Learning Languages*. Cambridge: Cambridge University Press.

West, Michael J. and Richard Donato. Fall 1995. "Stories and Stances: Cross-Cultural Encounters with African Folktales." *Foreign Language Annals* 28 (fall).

CHAPTER 4

DEFINING PERFORMANCE: CLASSROOM-BASED ASSESSMENT

WYT = WYG, OR, "WHAT YOU TEST IS WHAT YOU GET"

As foreign language professionals we are making great advances in the way we teach our students. We strive to make them better equipped to speak, listen, read, and write in the foreign language; we want to show them the end product, not just the discrete elements of vocabulary words, verb tenses, and grammatical structures. The articulation of outcomes in the Language Learning Continuum and the development of new instructional tools to achieve those outcomes are two very important parts of the circle. To complete the circle, however, we must also re-examine the types of assessment that we use in the classroom. It is critically important to test our students in ways that allow them to demonstrate their ability to perform the outcomes described at each of the stages of the Language Learning Continuum.

Unlike achievement assessment, which measures language skills in limited contexts, performance assessment provides students with the opportunity to show what they can do. In this chapter we will examine the role of assessment in the foreign language classroom, discuss practical ways of administering performance assessments, and give examples of assessment tasks for the five stages of language learning. In addition, you will find ideas on how you might alter these tasks for the K-6 learner.

The portfolio is one way to organize the many different types of performance assessment tasks that we now ask our students to complete. What can seem a daunting and overwhelming task of setting up and maintaining a portfolio for each of your students can be simplified with a little preplanning and some guided forms that the students use to keep their own portfolios in order.

You will find these forms as well as tips on how to incorporate the portfolio into your classroom in this chapter, beginning on page 94. In addition, you will see how the portfolio can be used as a vehicle for communication with the students about their work, which in turn empowers them to take an active role in the process of language learning.

Another way to encourage students to be actively engaged in their learning is to share with them your clearly articulated expectations for their assessment tasks in the form of rubrics. Given the open-ended nature of performance assessment, rubrics are an essential tool. Rather than expecting our students to read our minds and know how we want them to perform, rubrics define that clearly, making it possible for all students to strive for excellence. In this chapter, you will find examples of different rubrics as well as practical advice on how to include rubric scores in a traditional grading system. Teaching your students to understand and work with rubrics also teaches them the invaluable skill of self-evaluation and reflection on their own work as well as the work of their peers. By encouraging our students to take an active role in their learning while they are in our classrooms, we hope to set them on the path of being lifelong learners when they leave the classroom setting.

Finally, in this chapter we will discuss an assessment tool that is useful to demonstrate students' completion of one stage of language learning and advancement into the next one: integrated assessment. This is an assessment that integrates the skills of speaking, listening, reading, and writing in performance assessment tasks based on a central theme or topic. Through explanation and examples, you will see how integrated assessment, administered at any time of year when you feel your students are completing a stage, is essential to provide important information to students, teachers, administrators, and parents about the students' progress through the Language Learning Continuum.

Assessment Tasks

Standardized and Achievement Tests

For well over a hundred years standardized testing has played an integral part in the educational practice of the United States. Before the education reform movement of the early 1990s, standardized testing was one of the most commonly adopted and broadly administered types of testing among teachers, schools, districts, and states.

The first recorded standardized test in the United States can be traced to 1854, when the first written test was administered to supplement the traditional oral examination. During the early twentieth century, standardized tests served a number of purposes and gained much popularity. In the 1920s a new concept was added to standardized tests for measuring students' "achievement." With the development of the computer and machine scoring in the 1960s this additional dimension in standardized tests gained rapid momentum and popularity. Then, in the 1980s, achievement tests gained yet another new purpose when many states used them on a large scale to gather data to measure the quality of schools (Hymes, Chafin, and Gonder, 1991).

Standardized tests are usually developed by districts, states, or test publishers. They are administered to a large number of students under similar conditions in order to get comparable data. Among various standardized tests, the norm-referenced achievement test is the most commonly used by the schools. Norm-referenced testing is used to measure students' skills in different subjects; it allows an individual student or group of students to compare scores with those of the norm—a nationwide sampling of students who took the original test. Although comparing one student's scores against those of a norm does not reveal much about what the student knows, the users of standardized tests consider them of great value in educational practice: "Among the strengths of norm-referenced tests is the ability to measure a broad range of outcomes in a cost-effective, time-effective manner. This is in addition to their considerable strengths of reliability and validity" (Ibid). They are also considered the best instrument when periodically used to check students' achievement levels and to predict success. "Distinguishing among the knowledge, ability, and skill level of students is best done with a measure that compares student scores rather than one that tells what a student knows or doesn't know" (Ibid).

Another commonly administered standardized test is the criterion-referenced test. A criterion-referenced test usually consists of multiple-choice or essay questions designed to measure how well the student has mastered the curriculum objectives. This type of assessment measures individual student performance relative to explicit standards and provides reliable information concerning what a student has mastered and what remains to be mastered. One advantage of using criterion-referenced tests is that the test results clearly indicate to both the students and teachers what specific sets of skills need to be addressed. Many teacher-constructed classroom tests, such as quizzes, writing assessments, or projects are criterion-referenced. Even the more recently adopted alternative assessment approaches and techniques have been developed principally from the concept of criterion-referenced tests. The differences between criterion-referenced tests and alternative assessments lie mainly in their test purposes and approaches. Alternative assessments allow students to demonstrate to the best of their ability what they know and can do, and they also allow students and teachers the flexibility to choose the assessment methods.

The Importance of Alternative Assessment

The education reform movement in the 1990s has not only generated support to set higher curriculum standards nationwide, it has also become an impetus for creating different ways to assess a broader range of teaching and learning. Alternative assessments allow students to demonstrate their learning by choosing the topic, their partner(s), time element, materials, and the manner in which to "show off." In addition, they encourage teachers to assign more "real-life" tasks in which students exhibit learned skills and knowledge in simulated life situations.

Alternative assessments often include authentic assessment and performance assessment, and they distinguish themselves from traditional testing in many ways:

- They require open-ended, multidimensional, and high-cognitive approaches to measure students' complex cognitive abilities.
- They are not only pencil-and-paper tests; they require students to publicly perform, demonstrate abilities, develop projects, or defend their solutions.
- They allow students to select projects to demonstrate their mastery of material; they engage teachers and students in the evaluative process.
- They allow students to perform communication tasks in a natural context.
- They are not one-setting tests; they are conducted in many settings over a period of time in order to follow students' development.
- They view criteria as curriculum guides, not as curriculum objectives against which they are to be measured.
- They often involve students and teachers in planning assessment activities together.
- They are classroom-based assessments, so they take into consideration students' interests, abilities, and learning styles.
- Their emphasis is on collecting students' sample work at intervals to create reliable data for both students and teachers.
- They enable teachers to assess across the boundaries of different disciplines.
- They place equal weight on measuring students' learning processes and final products.

The *Standards for Foreign Language Learning* set five goals for foreign language education in the United States. Among the five goals, communication is undoubtedly the primary goal: "Communication, or communicating in languages other than English, is at the heart of second language study, whether the communication takes place face-to-face, in writing, or across centuries through the reading of literature" (*Standards*, p. 27). It is apparent that in teaching foreign languages, developing students' communicative proficiency should be the priority for every language teacher. In a classroom where communicative proficiency is being promoted, functional use of the language is the goal in curriculum design; grammar is embedded in contextualized language. Teachers create "authentic" instructional settings to prepare students to function in real-life situations, such as role-playing, asking for directions, making requests, or expressing feelings. The students in a proficiency-based classroom are allowed to advance at different rates because each individual student's learning ability, style, and pace have been taken into consideration. The students demonstrate what they can do with the language by giving oral presentations, constructing projects, making exhibitions, videotaping presentations, engaging in debates, holding interviews, etc. To cover the magnitude and complexity of what is going on in proficiency-based classrooms, traditional testing is often inadequate. A far better approach with which to evaluate proficiency-based classrooms is that of alternative assessment.

THE ADMINISTRATION OF PERFORMANCE-BASED ASSESSMENTS

One of the most commonly practiced assessment approaches is the performance-based assessment. Basically, in a performance-based assessment, students are required to "perform" a task individually or in a small group to demonstrate what they can do in a given situation. To maximize student performance, thorough preparation and thoughtful follow-up are a must.

Before administering performance-based assessment:

- Keep in mind that the assessment must be truly representative of classroom activities.
- Decide on a theme or topics related to the theme.
- Prepare students by relating the theme to their previously learned knowledge and skills.
- Introduce references to facilitate students' research if necessary.

- Suggest the length of time for preparation and presentation.
- Explain the entire process to the students.
- Set performance standards that are challenging but general enough to include all students.
- Set detailed performance guidelines that are clear.
- Let students know about the criteria for the performance, i.e., how to demonstrate competent performance by successfully blending specific knowledge and skills.
- Encourage students to integrate knowledge from other subject areas.
- Provide good examples so that students know what to strive for.
- Provide ample consultation for students.

During the administration of performance-based assessment:

- Students participate both as audience members and then as part of the evaluation process (during presentations).
- Each student's performance should be documented on audio- or videotape for the follow-up activity.

After the administration of performance-based assessment:

- Provide opportunities for individual/group discussion; allow students to self-evaluate/peer evaluate each other.
- Provide feedback that would enhance students' learning, e.g., how well they integrated their skills and knowledge, what needs further strengthening.
- Explain to the students whether or not they have met performance standards: accuracy, content, context, authenticity.
- Indicate to students how to improve their performance.
- Use all the information and data gathered to design the next learning experience for the students.

EXAMPLES OF ASSESSMENT TASKS FOR THE FIVE STAGES OF THE LANGUAGE LEARNING CONTINUUM

STAGE I

Each student prepares a "passport." Each passport contains the student's picture, name, date of birth, height, nationality, family/relatives, school name, grade, and his/her likes and dislikes. Students role-play a situation taking place at customs. Questions about self, places to visit, length of stay, items packed in luggage, etc., would be asked by the customs agent.

STAGE II

Each student prepares a "survival kit" for traveling to a country where the target language is spoken. This kit contains a self-made country/city map, an itinerary, plane and train schedules, places to visit and shop, types of native food and restaurant menus, lodging information, etc. Students demonstrate how to put their "survival kit" to use.

STAGE III

Each student demonstrates how to negotiate with someone in order to solve problems. Give students several simulated situations taking place while traveling in a country where the target language is spoken. For example: "You arrived at the hotel to find that there was no reservation made under your name and the hotel has no more vacancies." "The television in your hotel room does not work, but you were charged a fee for using it." "You need to switch to a nonsmoking room by convincing the manager that the air in the room is unbearable." Students create skits based on these problem-solving situations.

STAGE IV

Each student prepares an in-depth study of a topic relating to the target country that interests him/her the most. It can be a legend, the life story, or contributions made by a famous person; a cultural event or celebration that bears historical significance; a natural site or manmade structure that attracts tourists; a museum that houses precious art or artifacts; ancient or modern political/government structure; etc. Students use the target language to interview each other about their research.

Stage V

Show a videotape of a controversial issue taking place i͏ country where the target language is spoken. Newspaper ar written in the language can be substituted for this assessment activity if videotape is not available. Divide the students into two groups, each advocating an opposite view, and moderate a debate on the subject.

Adapting the Tasks for K-6 Learners

Many school districts have begun to offer foreign language programs beginning in kindergarten. It is important to note that although the focus of the Articulation and Achievement Project was not on the K-6 learner, the research and experiences garnered from working with students in grades 7-14 have many potential applications for the younger language learner, particularly the information related to Stages I and II. While the goals and many of the approaches for teaching this age group remain the same, assessment activities for the K-6 learners need to be modified due to developmental considerations.

Chittenden (1991) suggested a scope of assessment activities applicable to elementary education in his article "Authentic Assessment, Evaluation, and Documentation of Student Performance." His proposed assessment schema represents three different strands of evidence collected through multiple methods, namely, observation, performance samples, and a full range of devices for tests. Each strand is weighted equally in formulation or evaluation assessment practices. In applying Chittenden's assessment framework to K-6 learners in language classrooms, teachers are expected to gather students' performance evidence through the following assessment methods:

1. Teachers observe students' learning behavior such as:
   - students' everyday classroom participation
   - students' interest level
   - how students ask questions to each other and adult(s) in the room using the target language
   - how students respond to each other

These observations can be recorded in the form of checklists, rating forms, narrative descriptions, logs, and/or anecdotes.

2. Teachers collect students' performance samples through multiple methods that best demonstrate students' strengths and capabilities. These assessment tasks include reciting poems, singing songs, playing games, telephoning friends, giving prepared or improvised speeches, writing cards/notes/letters, incorporating language in arts-and-crafts projects, show and tell, performing skits, role-playing, mock interviews, etc. These performance samples can be documented by checklists, audio recordings, video recordings, logs, teacher's journals, and students' portfolios.

3. Teachers administer tests or test-like procedures, either commercially produced or teacher-constructed.

Helena Anderson Curtain and Carol Ann Pesola (1994) list key concepts for the younger learner in their book *Languages and Children—Making the Match*. They explain that the elementary or middle school learner performs best when the learning occurs in a meaningful context, and that while listening comprehension should be emphasized at first, speaking, reading, and writing (at age-appropriate levels) are also necessary for a successful language program. This strengthens the case for performance assessment at all levels, beginning with our youngest language learners.

SAMPLE ASSESSMENT ACTIVITIES FOR THE K-6 LEARNER:

SPEAKING

- Students volunteer in front of the class to make three statements and ask two questions that they have prepared ahead of time. If the topic pertains to themselves, they can make statements such as "I am 9 years old. I live in Connecticut. There are four people in my family. I like to sing and play basketball. Today I feel tired." Their questions can be on similar topics, such as "How old are you? Where do you live? How many people are in your family? What do you like to do? How do you feel today?" By asking for volunteers, the teacher can get the more confident students to go first, and to serve as models for the others.

- The teacher asks a few questions from a list that students have already prepared, and the student answers.
- Students choose several vocabulary items from a bag and say them in the target language.
- Students record audiotape monologues, dialogues, or songs that they have practiced.
- Students prepare and perform skits in front of the class. The teacher can assign a specific setting for the skit, and specific functions for the students to include. For example, the setting could be school, and the functions could be greeting each other, asking a few questions, and describing something. These skits can be videotaped.
- The teacher keeps a café or restaurant table set up somewhere in the room. Each day a pair or small group of students chooses a function or topic from a jar. They must go to the café and order a meal, in addition to talking about the topic or performing the function they have chosen.

Listening

- Students listen to the teacher's oral description and draw as many elements of it as they can. Ideas can include: a classroom, a person (including physical appearance and/or clothing), the weather, a kitchen, people doing various activities. A follow-up writing assessment can be to label a drawing they have done, perhaps with a word bank provided. The word bank can contain extra words that were not used in the original description.
- Given a drawing of several activities, each with a blank clock next to it, students listen to a description of when each activity takes place and then draw in the hands on the clock.
- Students are given a drawing of people in various locations doing several different activities. They listen to the teacher's statements about the drawing and write "yes" or "no" depending on whether each statement is true or false. Variation: students choose multiple-choice answers when asked about a drawing.

- Students label drawings, using words from a word bank.
- Students match phrases or short sentences with drawings.
- Students read a simple description and draw and color what is described. For example: a red square, a yellow star, etc.
- Students match vocabulary words in the target language with definitions in the target language.

A PRACTICAL GUIDE TO THE PORTFOLIO

The task of incorporating these many different types of assessments into each student's overall evaluation (whether it be a term, semester, or year grade), can be aided by the use of the portfolio. The portfolio is a tool that can be adapted to fit a variety of needs. At the same time it provides a way to categorize and organize the performance assessment tasks that are so important in today's foreign language classroom. In an ideal setting, students would be motivated by the goal of language proficiency, and grades would not be needed. However, in the reality of today's academic structure, we must assign grades to our students' work. In order to have that grade reflect the important goals of using the appropriate structures and vocabulary in reading, writing, listening, and speaking, a percentage of each student's grade is based on his or her portfolio work, which is a combination of a variety of assessment tasks performed that term.

Teachers of K-6 students often do not have to grapple with the same issues of assigning grades; however, for them the portfolio can also be a very powerful and reliable assessment tool. With younger students, when the assessment takes the form of projects, skits, drawings, or dialogues, the portfolio can provide a unique opportunity to group those tasks together in an organized and carefully planned way. One of the most important characteristics of the portfolio—the ability to track progress over time—can easily be illustrated through a selection of portfolio assessments adapted to the grade level of the learner. Imagine a videotape of a group of kindergarten students just learning their first words in a new language, juxtaposed with a tape of those same students in third grade performing a role-play in a restaurant scene! The possibilities are endless.

The concept of keeping a portfolio as a collection of a student's best work over time, and reflecting on it, is well-known to language professionals; however, this task can seem overwhelming to a teacher faced with five classes and a large number of students. What follows is an example of a system that can be set up to help organize the portfolio and make it manageable for teachers, while still being very beneficial to students.

As with any task, the process must begin with a clear articulation of goals. The Language Learning Continuum provides us with the guide as to where students are and where we want them to be. But the specific elements of the portfolio can be determined by the individual teacher. You can decide to include tasks from all four skills in your portfolio, or you can focus on one or two, depending on your own goals and the other types of assessment you administer. It is also necessary to determine how many tasks you will include in the portfolio for any given marking period; quantity is not as important as the type of task or the range of outcomes assessed by a certain task. By planning carefully and choosing your tasks wisely, your students can demonstrate their ability to perform in the language with four or five tasks per marking period. Once you have determined what to include, it is helpful to explain the portfolio process in a document that you can give to students and parents at the beginning of the school year. The following is an example of one such document used at the secondary level.

EL PORTAFOLIO EN LA CLASE DE ESPAÑOL

In this class, you will be keeping a portfolio of your written and spoken Spanish. The tasks you will perform will show how well you can actually use the language in a real-life context. Some tasks will be completed with the help of dictionaries, textbooks, partners, etc.; others will be completed using only what you know on your own. In the latter case, you will always receive advance warning of an upcoming portfolio task and the topics you should review in order to successfully complete it.

As you know, your portfolio work accounts for 30 percent of your term grade. During each term, you will complete a minimum of two speaking tasks and two writing tasks. They

---

will be graded using holistic criteria. You will be able to redo each writing task one time. Certain speaking tasks can also be done again. During terms 1 and 3, your portfolio grade will consist of an assessment of the four tasks done that term.

At the end of terms 2 and 4, you will have an opportunity to select and reflect on your best works from among all those done during the semester. You will write a self-evaluation, explaining why you chose what you chose, your strengths, weaknesses, and the progress you have made. You will then have a conference with me during which we will discuss your work and your evaluation. Thoughtful completion of the self-evaluation and the conference are part of the portfolio grade. Your portfolio will stay in the classroom until the end of the year, at which time you will take it with you to your next class.

It will include:

- both drafts of writing tasks with an evaluation sheet
- the evaluation sheet of speaking tasks
- a table of contents
- the criteria for evaluation
- your self-evaluations

At the end of the year, you will be able to look back and see the progress that you have made, and the following year, as you continue studying Spanish, you can continue to build on your ability to speak and write Spanish.

A key element of the portfolio process is the student's self-evaluation. Students often get back a quiz, a test, or a paper, look at the grade, read the comments (maybe) and put it away. For students to be active participants in their education, however, they must learn to look at their own work critically, and make thoughtful comments and insights that will help them improve their work rather than repeat the same mistakes again and again. Time constraints do not allow for conferences on a daily or weekly basis; so, in order to ensure that students remember why they did well or poorly on a particular assignment, what they liked or disliked about an assignment, or how they prepared for it, the self-evaluation process must take place immediately upon the return of each portfolio task. K-6 learners can also begin to self-evaluate their work with the help of a teacher who can record the students' thoughts and guide them in the process. The simple forms below can be used to facilitate that process and can be attached to the product and included in the portfolio.

The evaluation form also helps to organize the portfolio by including the title of the task, the term during which it was performed, and the scores (first and second draft) that the student received. A final organizational tool is the table of contents, which the student updates as each new task is added to the portfolio. A reminder from the teacher ("You should now have eight items listed in your table of contents.") can help keep even the most disorganized student on track!

When it is time for the portfolio conference, students prepare by referring to the comments they made on each self-evaluation sheet. It is often helpful to provide the student, especially one who is new to reflecting on his or her own work, with a guide or set of questions to prepare prior to the portfolio conference. At the K-6 level, rather than have them fill out a form, a preconference meeting with the teacher could get the students thinking about and planning for the upcoming conference. The K-6 conference could also be combined with regular parent conferences to provide younger learners with an opportunity to showcase their work.

Self-evaluation and reflection are skills that need to be taught and take time to learn; yet, once mastered, they are skills that will become invaluable to both teacher and students. By allowing students to express their opinions and share their views, they become more involved, enthusiastic and, as a result, more successful language learners.

Finally, it is important to work with your colleagues in designing your portfolios and determining the procedures you will use. Portfolios should be continued from year to year to show the progress as the student advances from one stage to the next on the Language Learning Continuum. Particularly since we know that a stage is not necessarily completed in an academic year, the portfolio, in order to faithfully illustrate a student's progress, must con-

EVALUATION FORM: WRITING TASKS

Name: _____

Task: _____

Date completed: _____

1st draft: Comments _____

_____

_____

_____

2nd draft: Comments _____

_____

_____

_____

Term: _____

Rating: _____

Teacher evaluation: _____

_____

_____

_____

Student's self-evaluation: _____

_____

_____

_____

INDICE DEL PORTAFOLIO

Task:	Date:	Rating:

CONFERENCIA DE PORTAFOLIO ENERO 19—

Please answer the following questions about your portfolio work for the first half of the year. We will meet during class sometime before the end of the term. Of the eight items that are in your portfolio, which four are your favorites? Explain why you are picking each one.

1. Task:

Why:

2. Task:

Why:

3. Task:

Why:

4. Task:

Why:

Look at the four items that you chose. Is there a balance between written and oral items? Why do you think it is that way?

What have you learned about writing and/or speaking Spanish from doing the portfolio work?

In which areas have you made improvements since the beginning of the year? In which areas do you still need to improve?

What do you like about the portfolio work?

What do you dislike about portfolio work?

Is there a type of activity or a specific topic/grammar point/vocabulary that you would like to focus on via a portfolio assignment? Explain.

Do you have any suggestions for activities (other than portfolio) that you would like to do between now and the end of the year?

Is there anything else you would like to add, either about your work or the class?

Nombre:

Fecha:

tinue from course to course. Ideally, a portfolio should stay with the student as he or she goes on to study at the postsecondary level as well, either as part of the admission process or to aid in the task of placing students appropriately as they begin studying at the new institution. There are certainly an abundance of applications for the portfolio, all of which aid in the overall goal of encouraging students to strive for proficiency and to continue to progress toward that goal throughout their years of formal study.

HOLISTIC SCORING AND RUBRICS

Participants in the Articulation and Achievement Project discussed at length and then practiced using holistic scoring techniques. Holistic scoring is a way of looking at and grading a student's work as a whole product, or performance. Individual errors are not counted or subtracted from a total. Instead, the teacher assesses the work as a whole, and bases the evaluation on the general impression of the strengths of the entire product.

Scoring rubrics are an essential part of holistic assessment. Rubrics clearly describe and specify the expectations for student work. Many different types of rubrics can be used, and new ones can be created with various point scales and different criteria, depending on the type of assignment and the teacher's expectations for it. In order for the rubrics to have relevance and meaning to students and parents, they must be shared with them. As Grant P. Wiggins (1993) states in his "Assessment Bill of Rights," "All students are entitled to...clear, apt, published, and consistently applied teacher criteria in grading work...[and to] minimal secrecy in testing and grading."

Using holistic scoring rubrics is not difficult; in fact, it can greatly simplify the grading process. However, a few important points need to be kept in mind. Holistic scoring is a criterion-referenced scoring technique. In other words, a student's work is compared only to the criteria, i.e., to the descriptors in the rubric. With holistic scoring, students can get a more complete, descriptive picture of their performance. They can better understand exactly where their strengths and weaknesses are, and how they can improve. Ideally, over time, students will see movement up the scale of the rubric as their work improves.

A rubric can be written as broadly or as specifically as needed. One rubric might be applicable for a wide variety of tasks, such as written essays, letters, spoken monologues, and paired dialogues. Another rubric might be written so that it is appropriate only for one particular assignment. During the course of the Articulation and Achievement Project, participants collaborated on and designed a general rubric that can be used for various types of both oral and written assessments. This rubric focuses on the question: Does this work exceed, meet, or not meet the expectations that the teacher has for this skill at this point in the course? (See pages 102-106 for this and other sample rubrics.)

At some point teachers will need to decide how to transfer rubric scores into a more traditional grading system in order to incorporate them into a term, semester, or year grade. In some cases, a rubric can be written so that a number score correlates to a traditional letter grade. However, in most cases a conversion system needs to be developed to reflect the wording of the descriptors and also to take into account the number of tasks that each student performed during the marking period. For instance, the "0, 1, 2, 3" scale used in the Articulation and Achievement Project does not transfer to letter grades in a straightforward manner. The 3 descriptor exemplifies what most teachers consider to be A work. The 2 descriptor, however, is broader, and encompasses both B and C work. Teachers in the project have used a 2+ and 2– to further define the scale to fit the needs created by a specific assessment task. The conversion method used should, of course, be explained to students. We do not want our students to think that a score of 2 on a three-point scale corresponds to a grade of D (2/3 = 67 percent).

The entire process of using holistic scoring techniques can be made clearer and more relevant to the students if they have a chance to participate in the task of writing and using rubrics. The teacher can describe a speaking or writing task, and then ask the students to design a rubric that would be appropriate for assessing it. This activity works well in groups, especially after the students have had a chance to read rubrics written by others. The groups need to decide which categories will be important for the task and how to describe them. For example, for a speaking task, they would need to discuss questions such as: Will pronunciation be considered in the evaluation? What about fluency?

Articulation and Achievement Rubric

3) Exceeds Expectation

- Message very effectively communicated
- Rich variety of vocabulary
- Highly accurate, showing no significant patterns of error
- Content supports interest level
- Self-correction increases comprehensibility

2) Meets Expectation

- Message generally comprehensible
- Vocabulary is appropriate, with some groping
- Accuracy appropriate to stage, although some patterns of error may interfere with comprehension
- Occasional self-correction may be successful

1) Does Not Meet Expectation

- Message communicated with difficulty and is unclear
- Vocabulary is often inappropriate, leading to miscommunication
- Significant patterns of error
- Content repetitious
- Self-correction is rare and usually unsuccessful

0) Unratable

- No consistent use of target language, only isolated words in target language
- Off task

Rubric for Student Portfolios

5) The task is completed fully in a creative way, and there is also additional information beyond the assignment. The work is organized and presented in a manner appropriate to the task. It is virtually free of grammatical errors. The vocabulary is sophisticated and is used in the correct way. Syntax is complex, demonstrating a willingness to take risks.

4) The task is completed fully. The work may be lacking in some small area of organization or presentation, but there are still paragraphs, transitions, etc. The minor grammatical errors do not interfere with communication and occur in structures less familiar to the student. The vocabulary is varied and is mostly used in the correct way. Syntax demonstrates complexity with some errors.

3) Some parts of the task are incomplete. The work lacks some major elements of organization and/or presentation. There are grammatical errors in both familiar and unfamiliar structures, but communication is still possible. The work demonstrates an understanding of basic vocabulary, with some errors in usage. Syntax is simple yet correct.

2) The work approaches the goal of the task but lacks several key elements. It is difficult to determine the organizational model for the work, which obscures the presentation. There are many grammatical errors in the work even in the basic structures, and parts of the work are difficult to understand. The basic vocabulary learned in class is often used incorrectly. Syntax is simple and sometimes incorrect.

1) The work almost completely misses the goal of the task. There is no organizational pattern. There are so many grammatical errors that communication is greatly obstructed. There is interference from the native language in grammatical structures, vocabulary and syntax.

0) Irrelevant or no response.

Source: J. Darias, 1996.

WRITING RUBRIC

EXCEEDS EXPECTATION

- Task Completion: Exceeds required elements.
- Communication of Message: Text comprehensible, appropriate, well-organized and with elaboration.
- Level of Expression: Consistent use of varied sentence structures with some transition words.
- Vocabulary: Rich use of vocabulary with frequent attempts at elaboration.
- Grammar: No, or almost no, grammatical, spelling, punctuation, and/or capitalization errors.

MEETS EXPECTATION

- Task Completion: Required elements present.
- Communication of Message: Text comprehensible, appropriate, and adequately developed.
- Level of Expression: Adequate use of varied sentence structure.
- Vocabulary: Adequate and accurate use of vocabulary for this level.
- Grammar: Some minor grammatical, spelling, punctuation, and/or capitalization errors.

ALMOST MEETS EXPECTATION

- Task Completion: Some required elements present.
- Communication of Message: Text mostly comprehensible, appropriate yet undeveloped.
- Level of Expression: Occasional use of varied sentence structures.
- Vocabulary: Somewhat inadequate and inaccurate use of vocabulary and too basic for level.
- Grammar: Frequent grammatical errors and errors in spelling, punctuation, and/or capitalization.

MINIMAL ATTEMPT TO MEET EXPECTATION

- Task Completion: Almost no required elements present.

- Communication of Message: Text barely comprehensible, frequently inappropriate.
- Level of Expression: Almost no variety in sentence structure.
- Vocabulary: Inadequate and inaccurate use of vocabulary.
- Grammar: Few correct grammatical structures with frequent errors in spelling, punctuation, and/or capitalization.

UNRATABLE/NO ATTEMPT TO MEET EXPECTATION

- Task Completion: No required elements present.
- Communication of Message: No attempt to convey message.
- Level of Expression: No attempt to use target language.
- Vocabulary: No attempt to use target language vocabulary.
- Grammar: No attempt to write in target language.

Source: Fairfax County Virginia Public Schools Foreign Language Program.

MORGAN SCHOOL (CLINTON, CT) INTERVIEW RUBRIC

6) THOROUGH COVERAGE OF A VARIETY OF TOPICS
- Responses to interview questions are thorough and cite many examples
- Interview questions display insight, relativity, and cultural awareness
- Accurate use of idioms and interesting vocabulary
- Expression is free of errors, effective and fluent

5) COVERS MANY TOPICS
- Responses to interview questions are thorough and cite examples
- Accurate use of vocabulary, correct spelling
- Accurate use of grammatical structures

4) COVERS SEVERAL TOPICS

- All of the responses adequately address the interview questions
- Accurate use of vocabulary, few spelling or grammatical errors
- Ideas are clear and understandable

3) COVERS A NUMBER OF TOPICS

- Most responses answer interview questions
- Some awkward use of vocabulary and spelling errors
- Grammatical mistakes are evident, but general meaning is comprehensible

2) ATTEMPTS TO COVER SEVERAL TOPICS

- Some responses address interview questions
- Inaccurate use of vocabulary and incorrect spelling
- Poor use of grammatical structures interferes with comprehension

1) FAILS TO COVER A VARIETY OF TOPICS

- Interviewee's answers do not address the interview questions
- Limited, inaccurate use of vocabulary and incorrect spelling
- Poor use of grammatical structures impedes meaning

Source: The Guide to K-12 Program Development in World Languages, First Draft, Connecticut State Department of Education, Division of Teaching and Learning, Bureau of Curriculum and Teacher Assessment, 1998.

How do we describe how comprehensible the speaker is? How do we describe how thoroughly the speaker completed the assignment? The teacher can give the students as much guidance as desired to point them in the right direction.

Once they have completed their rubrics, the groups can present them to the rest of the class, either on an overhead transparency, or photocopied for the following day. The groups can vote on a rubric to use, or work together to synthesize the best elements of all of them to create a new rubric. Then, keeping all of this work in mind, they can complete the speaking or writing task. Upon completion, they can then evaluate their work through self-assessment or peer assessment. Groups can be formed again, and each group can assess several students' work. This works well for writing tasks, especially if photocopies can be made, and for speaking tasks if they can be audio- or videotaped. Students get the opportunity to see the work of some of their classmates, and they get feedback from them about their own work. Similar self-, peer , or group evaluations can be carried out with a rubric of the teacher's choosing as well.

INTEGRATED ASSESSMENT

Traditionally, we have given our students examinations at the end of the academic year as a final determinant as to whether or not the student has passed the course. The exam might include items related to vocabulary and grammatical structures taught during the year, as well as reading comprehension and other activities. As has become evident from the work of the Articulation and Achievement Project, seat time in a classroom or even a passing grade for a course does not necessarily mean that a student has completed a stage in the Language Learning Continuum. Therefore, it is critical to assess students in such a way as to be able to demonstrate the successful completion of one stage and the advancement into the next one. Since this can occur at any time during the year (for example, students may complete Stage I in October of their second year of language study), unlike final examinations typically given in May/June, the assessment can be administered at any point during the year.

The integrated assessment is uniquely qualified to be a culminating activity for a stage because it combines the skills of speaking, listening, reading, and writing in performance tasks under one central theme or topic. The functions, context, and content evaluated in an integrated assessment correlate to the stage that the students have completed, thereby allowing them to demonstrate their ability to perform at a level that meets or exceeds the expectations of the stage in terms of text type and accuracy. A student who performs below expectation needs more time and assistance at the current stage before advancing on to the next stage.

An integrated assessment can be administered over several days of regular class periods or during an extended period if such a time slot is available. Students may be told the format of the assessment as well as the central theme or topic ahead of time, but they should not know the specific task until they begin the assessment. The criteria for evaluating the students' work should be articulated and shared with the students prior to the administration of the assessment as well. Speaking assessments can be done in a variety of formats, from face-to-face interviews to audiotaped or videotaped recordings. Once the administration of the actual assessment is complete, it is preferable to have more than one person evaluating each student's work, or to have someone other than the classroom teacher evaluate the work. As with the portfolio, it is essential that colleagues work together on this very important task.

The following is an example of an assessment given to a Stage III Spanish class.

RUNNING FOR CLASS PRESIDENT

STAGE III (SPANISH)

PART 1

Your school is about to begin elections to elect class officers. You're trying to decide if you want to run for class president. In order to find out more information about politics at your school, the role of the class officers, and the procedures for the campaign and the elections, read the following article published in your school newspaper. When you have finished, make some lists to help you in the decision-making process.

MAKE LISTS (IN ENGLISH) OF:
- the pros and cons of being involved in the politics of your school;
- the responsibilities of the class president;
- the responsibilities of the vice-president, secretary, and

treasurer of the class; and
- the schedule for the campaign and the elections.

PART 2

You have decided to run for president of your class! The school newspaper is running a special section in the next edition that will feature all the candidates. Each candidate must contribute a short biography for the section. In addition to writing about yourself and what you're like, make sure you describe past experiences you've had that make you the best candidate.

PART 3

There is so much to do when you are running for office. You have to make posters to hang in the corridors at school, buttons for your supporters to wear, and signs for people to carry outside. You also need to write speeches, and decide what promises you want to make and what you want to try to change. You have to do whatever is necessary to try to win the support of your classmates! Some of your friends have come over to your house today to help you with some of the work. Tell them what to do.

PART 4

While you were out working on your campaign, the faculty advisor of the class officers called to give you some important information on upcoming events. Listen to the answering-machine message and write down the following information:
- when you will be giving your election speech (day/time)
- which candidates will speak first, second, and so on
- where you will be giving your election speech
- how long your speech should be
- what you should wear on the day of the speech
- where and when the speech rehearsal will take place

PART 5

The election is coming up in a few days, and you have been very busy talking to your classmates to try to convince them to vote for you. You have just met a voter who has not yet decided who she is going to vote for. Talk to her and explain why you are the best candidate for class president.

PART 6

Tomorrow is the big day!! You will be giving your speech tomorrow. This is your last chance to show everyone that you are the best candidate. Write your speech, but remember to be brief. You don't want to bore any potential voters!! (No more than one page.)

Source: J. Darias, 1996.

As with all performance-based tasks, the students have the opportunity to show you what they can do with the language that they have been studying. A carefully designed integrated assessment can help you determine if your students have successfully completed the stage. The question remains, though, as to what to do with those students who are unable to meet or exceed the expectations of a given stage. If the majority of the students *cannot* successfully complete the integrated assessment, more work needs to be done at the current stage before advancement to the next is possible. If, on the other hand, a small number of students do not meet expectations, you may need to consider other options. Should they be asked to repeat a course or go to a course that has a slightly different approach? Should they simply continue where they are and be given another assessment at a later date? These are questions that are not easily answered, but ones that we as foreign language professionals need to address, particularly now when communities are demanding increasing accountability for the money they spend on education. In the end, we have to be able to help all our students learn to use the language and advance through the stages of the Language Learning Continuum.

Frequently Asked Questions

Don't these new performance-based assessments encourage "teaching to the test"?

Yes. When students and teachers know ahead of time what the assessment activities will be, teaching and learning will focus on the skills needed for success. However, performance-based assessments elicit complex, varied, and creative language samples, and in order to succeed at these assessments, students need more preparation than simply memorizing a particular word list or set of grammatical endings. A significant amount of classroom time must be devoted to actually practicing for the assessments, using structures and situations similar or identical to the formal assessment.

How can I supervise and manage the rest of the students in a classroom where one or more are involved in oral performance-based assessments?

There are several possibilities. Team up with another foreign language teacher who is free during your class, making arrangements for the colleague to either teach or administer the assessments (with the understanding that you will reciprocate). Establish department-wide assessment days, and collaborate with your colleagues to administer and score the assessments. Require all students to listen to the assessments of their classmates and, as a graded assignment, report (orally or in writing) on particular details they hear. Enlist the support of a student, student teacher, or colleague to audio- or videotape the assessments in a nearby room or hallway while the teacher remains in the classroom to monitor another activity, which can be interrupted when individuals leave the classroom for the oral assessment.

Do students who "fail to meet expectation" actually fail?

A student who fails to meet the expectation established in the rubric for any particular assessment does not necessarily fail the assessment. This indicator means that the student's work is not up to par, and needs revision; more research, or simply more study, may be needed as well. Individual teachers need to set the limits regarding revisions. When used to describe a student's total performance, the "fails to meet expectation" suggests that the student probably needs more time to acquire the knowledge and skills required at a given stage. Such a student could not reasonably be expected to succeed at a more advanced level.

In a conference with the student, discuss how his or her achievement was "below expectation," either in broad terms or focused in particular areas. Indicate how the student might practice the needed skills and offer opportunities, and a time frame to retake the assessments. In some cases, a teacher may prefer to request that the student audit all or part of the next course and retake the required assessments with the entire class.

Do you recommend student self-evaluation or peer evaluation?

When students use rubrics to evaluate their own work, they often take a fresh look at their product and make positive modifications, which may be more meaningful than teacher corrections because the students have internalized the requirements of the activity. Thus, self-evaluation of a first draft, prototype, or simulated performance assessment can lead directly to an improved final version.

Learners can also assist one another by using rubrics to evaluate their peers' work. Peer evaluation should be formative, in that the input of other students aids the learner in preparing the best possible assessment piece. It is important that a minimum of two peers evaluate each student's product, and it is best to assign evaluators in such a way that each student receives oral or written feedback from at least one conscientious, academically able classmate. Additionally, requiring students to submit self-evaluation and peer evaluation forms to the teacher may encourage them to reflect more carefully on their performance and feedback.

REFERENCES

Chittenden, Edward. 1991. "Authentic Assessment, Evaluation, and Documentation of Student Performance." In *Expanding Student Assessment*, edited by Vito Perrone. Association for Supervision and Curriculum Development, 22-30.

Curtain, Helena Anderson and Carol Ann Pesola. 1994. *Languages and Children—Making the Match*. White Plains, NY: Longman Publishing Group.

Darling-Hammond, Linda. 1994. "Performance-Based Assessment and Educational Equity." *Harvard Educational Review* 64, 1:5-30.

Diez, Mary, and C. Jean Moon. 1992. "What Do We Want Students to Know?...and Other Important Questions." *Educational Leadership* 49, 8:38-41.

Gardner, Howard. 1992. "Assessment in Context: The Alternative to Standardized Testing." In *Changing Assessments—Alternative Views of Aptitude, Achievement and Instruction*, edited by Bernard R. Gifford and Mary C. O'Connor. Boston: Kluwer Academic Publishers, 77-119.

Higgs, Theodore V., ed. 1984. *Teaching for Proficiency, the Organizing Principle*. Lincolnwood, IL: National Textbook Company.

Hymes, Donald L., Ann E. Chafin, and Peggy Gonder. 1991. *Testing and Assessment: Problems and Solutions*. American Association of School Administrators Critical Issues Report.

Jackson, Claire, et al. 1996. *Articulation and Achievement: Connecting Standards, Performance, and Assessment in Foreign Language*. New York: College Entrance Examination Board.

Kane, Michael B., and Ruth Mitchell, eds. 1996. *Implementing Performance Assessment: Promises, Problems, and Challenges*. Hillsdale, New Jersey: Lawrence Erlbaum.

National Standards in Foreign Language Education Project. 1996. *Standards for Foreign Language Learning: Preparing for the 21st Century*. Yonkers, NY: The National Standards in Foreign Language Education Project.

Padilla, Amado M., Juan C. Aninao, and Hyekung Sung. 1996. "Development and Implementation of Student Portfolios in Foreign Language Programs." *Foreign Language Annals* 29, 3:429-38.

Wiggins, Grant P. 1993. *Assessing Student Performance.* San Francisco: Jossey-Bass.

Wiggins, Grant P. 1992. "Creating Tests Worth Taking." *Educational Leadership* 49, 8:26-33.

Wiggins, Grant P. 1989. Teaching to the (Authentic) Test." *Educational Leadership* 46, 7:41-47.

Wolf, Dennie P., Paul LeMahieu, and Joanne Eresh. 1992. "Good Measure: Assessment as a Tool for Educational Reform." *Educational Leadership* 49, 8:8-13.

CHAPTER 5

AFTERTHOUGHTS: LESSONS LEARNED FOR HERE AND NOW

During the 1990s, the foreign language profession began to look more closely at the issues surrounding implementation of "proficiency-based" curricula and methods. One of the major questions that arose centered on which paradigm could best serve as a basis for articulation (or transition from level to level): a traditional grammatical paradigm, or the communicative paradigm provided by the ACTFL *Proficiency Guidelines* published in 1986. Teachers and administrators struggled with moving from a focus on grammatical competence to the instructional and organizational challenges posed by a curriculum based on communicative competence. They asked: If grammatical competence was deemed inadequate as a basis for student placement, how could appropriate benchmarks, derived from the Guidelines, be developed to create smoother transitions for students within, between, and among secondary and postsecondary institutions?

From this question, there arose several federal and state-supported projects whose goals were to establish learning standards based on the principles of linguistic competence and to define clearly what students should know, understand, and be able to do at the end of each stage of second language learning. What these projects contributed and what the Articulation and Achievement Project, in particular, learned, is the substance of this book.

The first chapter of *A Challenge to Change* points to the *Standards for Foreign Language Learning* (which evolved during the same period) as the beacon for developing and growing programs nationwide. It also recounts the efforts of teachers from middle schools, high schools, and postsecondary institutions seeking more effective ways to teach, to assess student growth, and finally, to build bridges for students as they move from level to level and from institution to institution as foreign language learners. The participating teachers, representative of most foreign language programs in New England, teach primarily in secondary schools and postsecondary institutions. Most teach in districts where second language study starts at grade 6 or 7. They know that language study that begins early and lasts for many years produces the best learners, and are interested primarily in answering two very present and practical questions: 1) Are there better strategies for teaching for proficiency when the language program does not begin in the early grades? 2) Are there better ways to encourage students who begin in grade 6 or 7 to continue their language study into college and beyond? The Language Learning Continuum developed from these questions. While each word in the phrase "language learning continuum" is important, the emphasis is on "continuum," suggesting the essential quality of continuous study over many years if real language acquisition is to take place.

COLLABORATIVE SCORING

As described in Chapter 2, the Language Learning Continuum emerged from the study of written and oral samples of students in the classes of teacher participants between 1993 and 1996. Each of the samples was evaluated using the generic rubric (see p. 102) in conjunction with descriptions of each stage in the continuum to determine the score. Each of the samples printed in this text was evaluated by at least two readers. If the first two readers' scores were inconsistent, the sample was read or listened to by a third reader for validation. One clear realization that emerged from this process, and which all participants will acknowledge, is the value not only of having the luxury of two or three readers but also of having the time to discuss individual judgments, to compare insights and opinions.

The collaborative nature of these discussions, which took place regularly throughout the project, enabled participants to gain a deeper understanding of the process and, through consensus, to become more accurate and precise in their evaluations. While clearly impractical on the daily level, we strongly recommend setting aside some time in department or grade level meetings to practice scoring collaboratively. The result will be greater consistency among teachers and a much clearer sense among students of what is expected from them as they progress from stage to stage.

A second recommendation, which emerges from the first, is that when engaging in collaborative scoring, it is helpful and productive to work with samples that do not reveal the names of students or their teachers. This can be accomplished if, for example, teachers designate a code for their classroom, and use the last four digits of students' phone numbers to identify their papers or tapes. The only identifying feature should be the stage number so that scorers can reference the appropriate stage criteria as defined in the Continuum. Following this practice helps to avoid scoring based on preconceived notions or past performance and guarantees that students in courses designated by Stages I to V are evaluated on the same basis without reference to whether students are middle school, high school, or college students. Participants were often surprised to discover that the age of students frequently contributed more to the length of the sample than to the overall quality.

STAGE III: AN APPARENT CONTRADICTION

Without doubt, the most important lesson we learned as the Language Learning Continuum evolved was derived from what project participants discovered in their study of Stage III. As has been mentioned, it is at Stage III that students begin in earnest to integrate each of the skills and learned vocabulary and begin to express their own meaning with greater ease. Project participants found that the attainment of Stage III requires determination on the part of students and, equally important, great patience and awareness on the part of teachers. As students begin to internalize the very complex components of their new language, they naturally attempt to use it in increasingly sophisticated and original ways. As they do so, the relative accuracy that accompanied their performance when using memorized words, phrases, and short sentences in Stages I and II seems to dissipate, often with disappointing results. This apparent contradiction—greater inaccuracy at a higher stage of language acquisition—is a real phenomenon that teachers in the Articulation and Achievement Project clearly recognized but had not fully understood until faced with hundreds of student samples from nearly two dozen secondary and postsecondary sites. It is not by chance that this common reality frequently coincides with the point at which attrition levels are the highest, in grades 10 and 11.

The lessons we learned from this particular discovery are that it is extremely important to recognize that apparent carelessness or poor study habits at this stage may actually be, and often are, signs of growth, and that it is important for us as teachers to help students monitor their own language production and self-correct. At the same time, we must encourage students to keep on writing and speaking as much as possible. In classrooms where there is too much emphasis on accuracy over meaning, students often become discouraged and give up language learning altogether. In classrooms where there is too little emphasis on accuracy, students rarely gain the competence needed to move forward. Creating a balance where there is some tolerance for error as students struggle with increased language production is critical. In our experience, the accuracy of those students who are supported and encouraged to continue does improve as they approach Stage IV.

INTEGRATED CULTURE

The first publication about the results of the Articulation and Achievement Project contained no detailed information about how teachers in the project incorporated literature, history, and art into their instruction. At workshops and conferences since the mid-1990s, one of the questions that is nearly always asked is how to integrate these topics into a proficiency-based curriculum. The questions arose, we believe, because the role of literature, history, and art is not explicit in the Language Learning Continuum framework.

It may be useful to explain here that the decision not to be explicit was deliberate, since every attempt to incorporate more details resulted in endless lists of themes, topics, books, and people for each stage. As the lists grew longer, participants came to understand that there was no way to accomplish this goal while maintaining the instructional flexibility of the Continuum. Nevertheless, we have attempted in this publication to show, using well-recognized cultural materials, how nearly any work of literature, history, or art can and *should* be used in instruction, beginning with the earliest stages of language development. What we learned struggling with this question is the importance of the meaning of the term "content-based instruction." While not listing themes and topics, the Continuum suggests ways of making content accessible to students in a manner consonant with the level of their language development. Chapter 3 offers concrete suggestions for doing so with examples drawn directly from teachers' experiences.

CURRICULUM, INSTRUCTION, ASSESSMENT: FULL CIRCLE

Perhaps the greatest lessons learned in this project were drawn from our efforts to develop relatively simple classroom-based assessments that would reveal not only levels of student achievement, but also student growth over time. In Chapter 4, the writer describes a variety of ways to do this within the context of classrooms in the United States. The strategies described in this chapter were tried and greatly improved during the last three years of the project. In the beginning, our attempts to create fully descriptive student portfolios resulted in such a cumbersome product that the results created impossible challenges from the point of view of organization, storage, and more importantly, evaluation. Over time, the processes we imagined became more streamlined and simpler. We realized, for example, that a single well-formulated prompt could be used many times during the year. Doing so enables the teacher to witness growing sophistication, improved writing or speaking skills, and the growth of students' ability to monitor themselves and to self-correct when necessary.

THE INTERPRETIVE SKILLS

While emphasis has been placed in this text on speaking and writing because those skills produced the samples we used for analysis, listening comprehension and reading also played key roles in the development of the Continuum. Perhaps the most frequent observation from participants was how useful the Continuum was for their students' understanding, and consequently, their confidence relative to the interpretational mode. Once students fully understood (and trusted) that they probably wouldn't understand every word of a text (tape, video, or print) and that they were indeed not expected to understand every word, they gained confidence and were far more willing to engage a text head-on. Students learned instead to look and listen for recognizable words and phrases (Stage I), main ideas (Stage II), or main ideas with some supporting detail (Stage III). This realization led many participants to experiment more freely with authentic materials at the earliest stages and to incorporate these materials into student assessment on a regular basis.

UNDERSTANDING PROGRESS THROUGH ASSESSMENT

Comprehending, through assessment, what students actually know, really understand, and can effectively demonstrate facilitates both instructional and programmatic planning. If such assessment and instructional practices become institutionalized, and courses are planned to meet students at their level of competence, it seems reasonable to assume that more students will gain the confidence and the motivation to continue through the difficulties that accompany the acquisition of any worthwhile skill—from playing piano to solving complex mathematical problems. If, as was stated in the introduction to this book, performance and accountability are key words for education now and in the future, then perhaps some of the lessons learned in this project will be helpful to school districts and teachers everywhere who are at this moment engaged in the evaluation of past practice.

At the heart of what we learned is this: programmatic consistency and coherence do result in better learning. The

Language Learning Continuum can be used to provide a framework for programmatic consistency leading to smoother transitions for students within and between middle, secondary, and postsecondary institutions.

FROM THE NATIONAL PERSPECTIVE

The past 10 years in education may be characterized not so much by drastic change in methods and curriculum, but by repeated, occasionally strident, demands for better results. From the publication of *A Nation at Risk* in the early 1980s to the more recent widespread dissemination of the *Third International Mathematics and Science Study*, the growing public interest in and demand for increased accountability based on student performance has influenced and, in some cases, forced change. These changes, because they influence everything from state funding formulas to local curricula, have been and will continue to be debated at every level, bringing attention to all aspects of American education. In many ways, this book has similar goals; even its title, *A Challenge to Change*, suggests that alterations and modifications to current practice can result in improved results.

The ideas presented in this volume point to the issues at the center of the challenges we as a profession face as we enter the twenty-first century. While we have focused on instructional strategies, and in particular on classroom-based assessment, it is not possible to consider these issues outside the context of the challenges we face as a profession as a whole. These challenges include developing K-12 sequences for all students, providing a sufficient number of well-prepared teachers to teach the growing number of students, implementing rich professional development opportunities for existing and future staff, and continuing to find more effective ways to meet the instructional needs of students currently enrolled in foreign language programs nationwide. Even as we progress toward more K-12 programs, acquire new technologies for teaching languages, improve curricula, and consider alternative classroom-based assessment strategies, we must continue to strive for better ways to achieve our professional goals.

K-12 Foreign Language Programs

The first challenge is to the nation as a whole: to implement language instruction for all children in all schools in the United States, beginning in kindergarten and continuing through high school and beyond. During the mid-1990s, while the *Standards for Foreign Language Learning* were being written and a consensus had been reached nationwide among foreign language professionals to frame both national and state standards documents in the context of K-12 education, many in the profession hoped, and perhaps even believed, that the sheer common sense of a K-12 foreign language curriculum would lead to the development of well-funded programs. Although the numbers of elementary school programs have since that time continued to grow, they have done so at an exceedingly slow rate, one district at a time, and often without adequate funding or support to ensure integrity and longevity.

On a positive note, the trend in state standards throughout the country has been to include foreign language among the core subjects in developing state curriculum frameworks. These statewide efforts, while lacking adequate financial support to back them up at the local level, reflect a growing understanding of the need to introduce language learning early and to continue that study as long as possible. In addition, and perhaps more important, they represent an understanding that we are living in an increasingly multicultural world driven by a global economy. The future of foreign language education is inevitably linked to the policies that will support and fuel this economy. As Jeffrey Munks, an executive in the Government Affairs office of ATT and a member of the Advisory Committee to the National Standards Project, asserts, foreign language teachers and American policymakers need to: first, find a way to work together to improve the teaching of languages; second, grow market opportunities for language services; third, promote language uses for education, government, business, and the community; fourth, develop a national language policy for the United States; and finally, improve both national capacity and supply for languages other than English (Munks, 1996).

Meeting these five objectives will require more sustained, comprehensive, and collaborative efforts than we have exerted in the past because we have not yet succeeded in achieving national consensus about the critical nature of second language learning in the United States. Once there is such consensus, the journey forward will progress. As an example of how this occurs, let us look for a moment at what has happened over the past 10 years with the entry of technology into the school curriculum. While there are great differences among schools in the depth and richness of their infrastructure, every school district in the United States is currently engaged in major efforts to purchase classroom computers and software and to link every child to the Internet. Computer equipment and staffing have become essential district expenditures, adding as much as 1 to 2 percent to the base of school district budgets throughout the country.

The need for new technologies in the twenty-first century is compelling; technological competence is correctly perceived as an integral part of American life and economy. Without such competence it is difficult to enter the work force, to continue one's education, or to interact with the rest of the world on a personal or a business level. In other words, technology has actually altered American culture. From the educational perspective it is, quite simply, a disadvantage not to be "plugged in." We might also ask: Is it a disadvantage not to know more than one language? Clearly, the American public understands that it is an advantage to know a second language, but they are not convinced that *it is a disadvantage not to know one*. For this reason, working at the local level to persuade taxpayers to spend that marginal dollar on elementary foreign language programs needs to become central to our work as advocates for foreign language instruction. We have already developed national standards and many individual state frameworks that support K-12 language instruction. We need to work toward realizing the political momentum necessary to fund language programs, to encourage better teacher preparation, and to support curriculum development; in other words, to reach the goals we established for students nationwide when the *Standards* were published.

EXCELLENCE IN TEACHING AND PRE-SERVICE PREPARATION

As a result of research and improved teacher training over the past 10 years, student teachers and new teachers currently working in the middle and secondary schools are now more likely to see themselves as facilitators and guides for students along the journey toward communicative proficiency; they have been immersed in the study of "proficiency-oriented instruction" and are aware of sound instructional practice. Pre-service education is successfully preparing student teachers to understand the complexities of Special Education, to respect the value of teaching language in context, to understand the needs of heritage language learners, and to be sensitive to and aware of the integrated nature of language and culture. These efforts are having a positive impact on the students, schools, and districts where these new teachers work. In fact, thanks to the work of colleagues at the postsecondary level, pre-service education has perhaps never been better. At the same time, as research at the National Center for Education Statistics reveals, the number of potential teachers is declining annually—a fact we have not yet adequately addressed (see the NCES Web site at nces.ed.gov).

As we succeed in developing support for K-12 programs, we must also succeed in preparing the teachers who will teach in those classrooms. Part of the challenge is represented by the fact that filling both new and current positions is becoming increasingly difficult. The demand for language teachers has risen gradually over the past 10 years, and many department chairs, principals, and central office administrators at the K-12 level are currently experiencing difficulty filling openings with qualified teachers to meet the demand for current programs. Districts in North Carolina, Virginia, and New Jersey have had to search outside the country to fill teaching positions created as a result of implementation of K-12 programs. In 1993, Nancy Rhodes and Audrey Heining-Boynton noted the shortage of trained elementary foreign language teachers, inadequate elementary foreign language preparation, and the general shortage of qualified teacher educators in North Carolina (p. 156). What was a statewide reality in the early 1990s has now reached national proportions. The trend raises serious questions. How should we direct our energies in the next 10 years? If, as experience and data suggest, the number of available teachers is declining, should we not be expending as much energy on rekindling an interest in teaching even as we advocate for new, expanded programs?

THE CHALLENGE OF PROFESSIONAL DEVELOPMENT

If the number of programs continues to increase, and if at the same time the number of foreign language teachers increases, schools, school districts, and professional language associations will have to turn their attention to developing coherence at the local, state, and national levels. In the mid-1980s, the publication of the ACTFL *Proficiency Guidelines* created an environment that encouraged the entire profession to renew itself. Nearly everything written during that period references the importance of communicative competence in a "proficiency" context. Perhaps K-12 foreign language education will provide the next consensus-building motif in the profession. If this does occur, it will become increasingly important to provide substantive and ongoing professional development for foreign language teachers. In addition to strong backgrounds in language, literature, culture, history, and art, foreign language educators will need to acquire a deeper understanding of the principles of language acquisition, including the practical need for well-articulated programs that are designed to ensure smooth transitions for students as they as proceed along the Language Learning Continuum.

PROFESSIONAL CROSSROADS

Since the early 1980s, the United States has been engaged in a comprehensive examination of the strengths and weaknesses of our educational system. Foreign language educators have played an important and effective role in the final determination of what has been deemed essential in the definition of core curricula. The United States Department of Education supported the development of the *Standards for Foreign Language Learning* and their publication in 1996. In 1996, over 20 states had formally recognized proficiency in a language other than English as one of the core values at the center of state content standards

(Sandrock, 1996) and many included K-12 foreign language programs as part of their state education reform legislation. All in all, this has been a very encouraging decade for the foreign language profession. We have broken the "core curriculum" barrier, but there remain many equally and perhaps more challenging barriers to break as we enter the new millennium.

Now, looking back on the fullness and excitement of the twentieth century and ahead to the still vaguely defined promise of the twenty-first, we have a unique opportunity to evaluate the progress the profession has made and to signal those issues that remain to be addressed. The foreign language profession reinvented itself during the 1980s by learning about and implementing new instructional methods that moved the center of attention in second language learning from grammatical to communicative competence. This was accompanied by a growing awareness of the holistic nature of language and the improbability of developing competent learners by focusing on one aspect of language and literacy to the exclusion of others. In short, we found better, more effective ways to develop curricula and more effective ways to teach.

DOING IT RIGHT

A Challenge to Change: The Language Learning Continuum is about effective instruction leading to communicative proficiency and literacy on the part of the students we teach. In particular, *A Challenge to Change* aims to answer the question, "How do we get there from here?" Language teachers are currently studying the *Standards*, state frameworks, local curriculum documents, and our own practice in order to respond to this question. Guided by experience and the concepts of communicative proficiency, we are improving our understanding of the intricate relationships between teaching for proficiency, new ideas about modes of communication and assessment, methods for measuring and describing student competence, and well-articulated programs. By providing a practical lens though which to view the multifaceted task ahead, the Language Learning Continuum guides us into a way of thinking about student progress that can be used, with modifications, for any program beginning at any point of entry at the elementary, secondary, or postsecondary level. In addition, it is a yardstick with which we can define common measures for the effectiveness of student learning as well as the effectiveness of local programs.

Success will necessitate both a familiarity with and a deep understanding of all the changes that are occurring within the profession and outside. The first and perhaps the most important change in the professional landscape is the *Standards*. Intended as a document for a wide variety of audiences, this effort significantly strengthens, reshapes, and expands the way we have understood foreign language instruction up to now. The *Standards* describe the ideal—what is needed to do the right thing and what is needed to do it right. Our professional *Standards* are written to reflect the essential nature of long and uninterrupted sequencing in foreign language programs. The goals of communicative proficiency: cultural knowledge, learning about and connecting with other disciplines, deepening understanding of one's first language, and using the target language in real settings, are achievable in an educational setting that ensures articulated, consistently effective instruction. It is precisely because of the nature of language acquisition that a focus on matching instruction to students' levels of competence is critical. The difference between success and failure is in how we teach, the goals we set, and the instructional and programmatic accommodations made to recognize the level of student competence.

As Dulay, Burt, and Krashen point out in their book entitled *Language Two:*

> Learning a second language can be exciting and productive...or painful and useless. One's efforts can end in the acquisition of native-like fluency or a stumbling repertoire of sentences soon forgotten.

> The difference lies in how one goes about learning the new language and how a teacher goes about teaching it. To be successful, a learner need not have a special inborn talent for learning languages. Learners and teachers simply need to "do it right." (1982, p. 3)

For that reason, the effort to constantly seek new and better ways to teach, to motivate learners, and to provide the best environment for success defines what "doing it right" means today and will mean tomorrow. The Articulation and Achievement Project succeeded in answering certain aspects of the question posed at the beginning of this chapter. If grammatical competence is inadequate as a basis for student placement, how can appropriate benchmarks be developed to create smoother transitions for students within, between, and among secondary and postsecondary institutions? Much more work remains to be done. More fundamental questions about curriculum and instruction, scheduling, and length of sequence remain to be asked. The experience of the participants in the Articulation and Achievement Project suggests not only that the questions will be asked, but that they will be answered. Each answer will lead us closer to a nation of multilingual citizens who are fully prepared to engage in an economically interdependent global society.

Note to Readers: Several prepublication reviewers pointed out two facts: first, that the Language Learning Continuum was inconsistent with the K-12 goals and objectives of the *Standards* document since it addresses only grades 7-14, and that the language used in the stage descriptors did not include the words "presentational," "interpersonal," or "interpretive." These descriptors emerged during the *Standards* process, which began in the final year of the Articulation and Achievement Project. Project participants believe that the *Standards* K-12 set the stage for where we want to be; the Language Learning Continuum defines a better way for teaching in the context where most of us find ourselves now. The addition of the "modes" of language learning ("presentational," "interpersonal," and "interpretive") to the *Standards* provides a new and important dimension to the ways in which we look at language acquisition. These terms may be easily applied to the Language Learning Continuum as appropriate.

REFERENCES

Dulay, Heidi C., Burt, Marina, and Krashen, Stephen. 1982. *Language Two*. New York: Oxford University Press.

Munks, Jeffrey J. 1996. "The Case for Multilingual Citizens in the 21st Century." *Foreign Languages for All: Challenges and Choices*. (The Northeast Conference Reports.)

Rhodes, Nancy C., and Heining-Boynton, Audrey L. 1993. "Teacher Training with a Twist: A Collaborative Project in North Carolina." *Foreign Language Annals* 26 (2).

Sandrock, P. 1996. "State Foreign Language Standards Projects—A Sampling." *Foreign Languages for All: Challenges and Choices*. (The Northeast Conference Reports.)

.

BIBLIOGRAPHY

Note: The list below does not claim to be exhaustive. It does represent, however, those books and articles that had a direct or indirect impact on the project and that contain practical and readable information that the writers believe would be of interest to language teachers of all levels.

GENERAL

American Council on the Teaching of Foreign Languages. 1996. *Foreign Language Annals* 29 (fall). *Special Expanded Edition: Strategies and Techniques in Foreign Language Teaching.*

Birchbichler, Diane W., ed. 1990. *New Perspectives and New Directions in Foreign Language Education.* Lincolnwood, IL: National Textbook Company. (The ACTFL Foreign Language Education Series.)

Brecht, Richard D., and A. Ronald Walton. 1994. "The Future Shape of Language Learning in the New World of Global Communication: Consequences for Higher Education and Beyond." *In Foreign Language Learning: The Journey of a Lifetime,* edited by R. Donato and R.M. Terry. Lincolnwood, IL: National Textbook Company.

Byrnes, Heidi. 1984. "The Role of Listening Comprehension: A Theoretical Base." *Foreign Language Annals* 17, 317-29.

Donato, Richard and Robert M. Terry, eds. 1995. *Foreign Language Learning: The Journey of a Lifetime.* Lincolnwood, IL: National Textbook Company. (The ACTFL Foreign Language Education Series.)

Dvorak, Trisha, ed. 1995. *Voices from the Field: Experiences and Beliefs of Our Constituents.* Lincolnwood, IL: National Textbook Company. (The Northeast Conference Reports.)

Ervin, Gerard L., ed. 1991. *International Perspectives on Foreign Language Education.* Lincolnwood, IL: National Textbook Company. (The ACTFL Foreign Language Education Series.)

Friend, Marilyn and William Bursuck. 1996. *Including Students with Special Needs: A Practical Guide for All Teachers*. Boston, MA: Allyn and Bacon.

Guntermann, Gail, ed. 1993. Developing Language Teachers for a Changing World. Lincolnwood, IL: National Textbook Company. (The ACTFL Foreign Language Education Series.)

Hadley, Alice Omaggio, ed. 1993. *Research in Language Learning: Principles, Processes, and Prospects*. Lincolnwood, IL: National Textbook Company. (The ACTFL Foreign Language Education Series.)

Hadley, Alice Omaggio. 1993. 2nd ed. *Teaching Language in Context*. Boston, MA: Heinle & Heinle.

Hammerly, Hector. 1991. *Fluency and Accuracy: Toward Balance in Language Teaching and Learning*. Bristol, PA: Taylor and Francis, Inc.

Herron, Carol, and Irene Seay. 1991. "The Effect of Authentic Oral Texts on Student Listening Comprehension in the Foreign Language Classroom." *Foreign Language Annals* 24, 487-95.

Higgs, Theodore V., ed. 1984. *Teaching for Proficiency, the Organizing Principle*. Lincolnwood, IL: National Textbook Company. (ACTFL Foreign Language Education Series.)

Hirsch, Bette. 1989. *Languages of Thought: Thinking, Reading, and Foreign Languages. (The Thinking Series.)* New York: College Entrance Examination Board.

James, Charles J., ed. 1985. *Foreign Language Proficiency in the Classroom and Beyond*. Lincolnwood, IL: National Textbook Company. (The ACTFL Foreign Language Education Series.)

Jarvis, Gilbert A., ed. 1975. *Perspective: A New Freedom*. IL: National Textbook Company. (The ACTFL Review of Foreign Language Education Series, Vol. 7.)

Jurasek, Barbara S., and Richard T. Jurasek. 1991. "Building Multiple Proficiencies in New Curriculum Contexts." In *Building Bridges and Making Collaborations*, edited by June K. Phillips. Middlebury, VT: Northeast Conference on the Teaching of Foreign Languages.

Omaggio, Alice C. 1979. "Pictures and Second Language Comprehension: Do They Help?" *Foreign Language Annals* 12, 107-16.

Phillips, June K., and Eileen W. Glisan. 1988. "Teachers Working with Teachers: Becoming Proficient with Proficiency." In *New Challenges and Opportunities. Dimension: Languages '87*. Report of the Southern Conference on Language Teaching, 109-19.

Phillips, June K., and Jamie Draper. 1994. "National Standards and Assessments." In *Meeting New Challenges in the Foreign Language Classroom*, edited by Gale Crouse. Report of the Central States Conference on the Teaching of Foreign Languages. Lincolnwood, IL: National Textbook Company.

Ramler, Siegfried. 1991. "Global Education for the 21st Century." *Education Leadership* (April), 44-46.

Rieken, Elizabeth. 1993. *Teaching Language in Context Workbook*, 2nd ed. Boston, MA: Heinle & Heinle.

Rissel, Dorothy. 1995. "Learning by Doing: Outcomes of an Overseas Summer Project for Teachers." *Foreign Language Annals* 28 (spring).

Stevick, Earle. 1988. *Teaching and Learning Languages*. Cambridge: Cambridge University Press.

The University of Kansas Institute for Research in Learning Disabilities. 1990. "The Strategic Instruction Model." Lawrence, Kansas: University of Kansas Institute for Research in Learning Disabilities.

Valette, Rebecca M. 1993. "The Challenge of the Future: Teaching Students to Speak Fluently and Accurately." *Canadian Modern Language Review* 50, 1: 173-78.

Wing, Barbara H., ed. 1996. *Foreign Languages for All: Challenges and Choices*. Lincolnwood, IL: National Textbook Company. (The Northeast Conference Reports.)

Language Acquisition

"Fertile Minds." *Time*, February 3, 1997, 49-56.

Hadley, Alice Omaggio, ed. 1993. *Research in Language Learning: Principles, Processes, and Prospects*. Lincolnwood, IL: National Textbook Company.

Holobow, Naomi E., et al. 1987. "Effectiveness of Partial French Immersion for Children from Different Social Class and Ethnic Backgrounds." *Applied Psycholinguistics* 8, 137-52.

Krashen, Steven, and Tracy Terrel. 1983. *The Natural Approach*. Hayward, California: Alemany Press.

Larsen-Freeman, Diane, and Michael H. Long. 1991. *An Introduction to Second Language Acquisition Research*. New York: Longman.

O'Mally, J. Michael , and Anna Uhl Chamot. 1990. *Learning Strategies in Second Language Acquisition*. Cambridge: Cambridge University Press.

Richard, Patricia A. 1996. *Making It Happen: Interaction in the Second Language Classroom: From Theory to Practice*. White Plains, NY: Amato, Longman.

Savignon, Sandra J. 1997. *Communicative Competence: Theory and Classroom Practice*. 2nd edition. New York: McGraw-Hill.

Assessment

American Council on the Teaching of Foreign Languages. 1986. *ACTFL Proficiency Guidelines*. Yonkers, NY: ACTFL.

Bachman, L.F. 1990. *Fundamental Considerations in Language Testing*. New York: Oxford University Press.

Bartz, Walter H. 1991. "Are They Learning What We're Teaching? Assessing Language Skills in the Classroom." In *Focus on the Foreign Language Learner: Priorities and Strategies*, edited by Lorraine A. Strasheim. Report of Central States Conference on the Teaching of Foreign Languages. Lincolnwood, IL: National Textbook Company.

Bloom, Benjamin, George Madaus, and John T. Hastings. 1981. *Evaluation to Improve Learning*. New York: McGraw-Hill.

Brecht, Richard, and Dan Davidson. 1992. "Language Acquisition Gains in Study Abroad: Assessment and Feedback." In *Language Assessment for Feedback: Testing and Other Strategies,* edited by Elana Shohamy and A. Ronald Walton. Dubuque, IA: Kendall/Hunt Publishing Co.

Byrnes, Heidi, and Michael Canale, eds. 1987. *Defining and Developing Proficiency: Guidelines, Implementations and Concepts.* Lincolnwood, IL: National Textbook Company. (The ACTFL Foreign Language Education Series.)

Chittenden, Edward. 1991. "Authentic Assessment, Evaluation, and Documentation of Student Performance." In *Expanding Student Assessment,* edited by Vito Perrone. Alexandria, VA: Association for Supervision and Curriculum Development, 22-30.

Connecticut State Department of Education. 1998. "Guide to K-12 Program Development in World Languages." Hartford, CT: State Department of Education, Division of Teaching and Learning, Bureau of Curriculum and Teacher Assessment.

————. 1990. "Toward a New Generation of Student Outcome Measures: Connecticut's Common Core of Learning Assessment." Hartford, CT: State Department of Education, Research and Evaluation Division.

Darling-Hammond, Linda. 1994. "Performance-Based Assessment and Educational Equity." *Harvard Educational Review* 64, 1: 5-30.

Diez, Mary and C. Jean Moon. 1992. "What Do We Want Students to Know?...and Other Important Questions." *Educational Leadership* 49, 8: 38-41.

Gardner, Howard. 1992. "Assessment in Context: The Alternative to Standardized Testing." In *Changing Assessments: Alternative Views of Aptitude, Achievement and Instruction,* edited by Bernard R. Gifford and Mary C. O'Connor. Boston: Kluwer Academic Publishers, 77-119.

Genessee, Fred and John A. Upshur. 1996. *Classroom-Based Evaluation in Second Language Education.* Cambridge: Cambridge University Press.

Hancock, Charles, ed. 1994. *Teaching, Testing, and Assessment: Making the Connection.* Lincolnwood, IL: National Textbook Company. (The Northeast Conference Reports.)

Higgs, Theodore V., ed. 1984. *Teaching for Proficiency, the Organizing Principle.* Lincolnwood, Illinois: National Textbook Company. (The ACTFL Foreign Language Education Series.)

Hymes, Donald L., Ann E. Chafin, and Peggy Gonder. 1991. *Testing and Assessment: Problems and Solutions.* American Association of School Administrators Critical Issues Report.

Jackson, Claire, et al. 1996. *Articulation and Achievement: Connecting Standards, Performance, and Assessment in Foreign Language.* New York: The College Entrance Examination Board.

Kane, Michael B., and Ruth Mitchell, eds. 1996. *Implementing Performance Assessment: Promises, Problems, and Challenges.* Hillsdale, New Jersey: Lawrence Erlbaum Associates.

Liskin-Gasparro, Judith. 1987. *Testing and Teaching for Oral Proficiency.* Boston, MA: Heinle and Heinle.

Marzano, Robert J., Bebra Pickering, and Jay McTighe. 1993. *Assessing Student Outcomes: Performance Assessment Using the Dimensions of Learning Model.* Alexandria, VA: Association for Supervision and Curriculum Development.

Medley, Frank. 1985. "Designing the Proficiency Based Curriculum." In *Proficiency, Curriculum, Evaluation: The Ties That Bind,* edited by Alice C. Omaggio. Middlebury, VT: Northeast Conference on the Teaching of Foreign Languages.

Padilla, Amado M., Juan C. Aninao, and Hyekung Sung. 1996. "Development and Implementation of Student Portfolios in Foreign Language Programs." *Foreign Language Annals* 29, 3:429-438.

Performance-Based Learning and Assessment. 1996. Southbury, CT: Pomperaug Regional School District No. 15.

Terry, Robert M. 1986. "Testing the Productive Skills: A

Creative Focus for Hybrid Achievement Tests." *Foreign Language Annals* 19, 6:521-30.

Wiggins, Grant P. 1993. *Assessing Student Performance: Exploring the Purpose and Limits of Testing.* San Francisco: Jossey-Bass.

———. 1992. "Creating Tests Worth Taking." *Educational Leadership* 49, 8:26-33.

———. 1991. "Standards, Not Standardization: Evoking Quality Student Work." *Educational Leadership* 48, 5: 18-25.

———. 1989a. "A True Test: Toward More Authentic and Equitable Assessment." *Phi Delta Kappan* 70, 9: 703-13.

———. 1989b. "Teaching to the (Authentic) Test." *Educational Leadership* 46, 7: 41-47.

———. 1988. "Rational Numbers: Scoring and Grading That Helps Rather Than Hurts Learning." *American Educator* 12, 4: 20-48.

———. 1987. "Creating a Thought-Provoking Curriculum." *American Educator* 11, 4.

Wolf, Dennie P., Paul G. LeMahieu, and Joanne Eresh. 1992. "Good Measure: Assessment as a Tool for Educational Reform." *Educational Leadership* 49, 8: 8-13.

Wolf, Dennie P. and Nancy Pistone. 1991. *Taking Full Measure: Rethinking Assessment Through the Arts.* The Thinking Series. New York: The College Entrance Examination Board.

National Standards

Harper, Jane, Madeline Lively, and Marianne Williams, eds. 1998. *The Coming of Age in the Profession.* Boston: Heinle & Heinle.

Lafayette, Robert C., ed. 1996. *National Standards: A Catalyst for Reform.* Lincolnwood, IL: National Textbook Company. (The ACTFL Foreign Language Education Series.)

National Standards in Foreign Language Education Project. 1996. *Standards for Foreign Language Learning: Preparing for the 21st Century.* Yonkers, NY: The National Standards in Foreign Language Education Project.

Phillips, June K., ed. 1997. *Collaborations: Meeting New Goals, New Realities*. Lincolnwood, IL: National Textbook Company. (The Northeast Conference Reports.)

Wolf, Dennie P. 1994. "Curriculum and Assessment Standards: Common Measures or Conversations?" In *The Future of Education: Perspectives on National Standards in America*, edited by Nina Cobb. New York: The College Entrance Examination Board, 85-106.

CULTURE AND LANGUAGE

Abrate, Jayne E. 1993. "French Cuisine in the Classroom: Using Culture to Enhance Language Proficiency." *Foreign Language Annals* 26, 1:31-37.

Allen, Wendy, Keith Anderson, and Léon Narváez. 1992. "Foreign Languages Across the Curriculum: The Applied Foreign Language Component." *Foreign Language Annals* 25:11-19.

Arries, Jonathan F. 1994. "Constructing Culture Study Units: A Blueprint and Practical Tools." *Foreign Language Annals* 27, 4:523-34.

Bacon, Susan M. 1995. "Coming to Grips with the Culture: Another Use of Dialogue Journals in Teacher Education." *Foreign Language Annals* 28 (summer).

Bacon, Susan M. Cameron. 1987. "Mediating Cultural Bias with Authentic Target-Language Texts for Beginning Students of Spanish." *Foreign Language Annals* 20, 6:557-63.

Brière, Jean-François. 1986. "Cultural Understanding through Cross-Cultural Analysis." *The French Review* 60, 2:203-08.

Brooks, Nelson. 1968. "Teaching Culture in the Foreign Language Classroom." *Foreign Language Annals* 1, 3: 204-17.

Byrnes, Heidi, ed. 1992. *Languages for a Multicultural World in Transition*. Lincolnwood, IL: National Textbook Company.

Carr, Tom. 1985. "Contemporary Culture: A Model for Teaching a Culture's Heritage." In *Meeting the Call for Excellence in the Foreign Language Classroom*, edited by

Particia B. Westphal. Lincolnwood, IL: National Textbook Company, 71-83.

Crawford-Lange, Linda M., and Dale L. Lange. 1984. "Doing the Unthinkable in the Second-Language Classroom: A Process for the Integration of Language and Culture." In *Teaching for Proficiency, the Organizing Principle*, edited by Theodore V. Higgs. Lincolnwood, IL: National Textbook Company. (The ACTFL Foreign Language Education Series.)

Damen, Louise. 1987. *Culture Learning: The Fifth Dimension in the Classroom*. Reading, MA: Addison-Wesley.

Failoni, Judith Weaver. 1993. "Music as a Means to Enhance Cultural Awareness and Literacy in the Foreign Language Classroom." *Mid-Atlantic Journal of Foreign Language Pedagogy* 1:97-108. (A publication of the Maryland Foreign Language Association.)

Foreign Language Annals Special Edition: The Teaching of Culture. Spring 1996. Vol. 29, no. 1.

Galloway, Vicki B. 1992. "Toward a Cultural Reading of Authentic Texts." In *Languages for a Multicultural World in Transition*, edited by Heidi Byrnes. Lincolnwood, IL: National Textbook Company, 87-121.

Garcia, Carmen. 1991. "Using Authentic Reading Texts to Discover Underlying Sociocultural Information." *Foreign Language Annals* 24, 6:515-26.

Gibaldi, Joseph, ed. 1992. *Scholarship in Modern Languages and Literatures*, 2nd ed. New York: Modern Language Association.

Gollnick, Donna M., and Phillip C. Chinn. 1994. *Multicultural Education in a Pluralistic Society*. Riverside, NJ: Macmillan.

Goodenough, Ward. 1981. *Culture, Language and Society*. Menlo Park, CA: Cummings.

Hahn, Sidney L. 1976. "Strategies for Increasing Cross-Cultural Awareness." In *Teaching for Communication in the Foreign Language Classroom*, edited by Renate A. Schulz. Skokie, IL: National Textbook Company, 65-92.

Hall, Edward T. 1976. *Beyond Culture*. New York: Doubleday.

Halverson, Rachel J. 1985. "Culture and Vocabulary Acquisition: A Proposal." *Foreign Language Annals* 18, 4:327-32.

Heusinkveld, Paula R. 1985. "The Foreign Language Classroom: A Forum for Understanding Cultural Stereotypes." *Foreign Language Annals* 18, 4:321-25.

Kramsch, Claire J. 1993. *Context and Culture in Language Teaching*. New York: Oxford University Press.

————. 1983. "Culture and Constructs: Communicating Attitudes and Values in the Foreign Language Classroom." *Foreign Language Annals* 16, 6:437-48.

Lado, Robert. 1957. *Linguistics Across Cultures: Applied Linguistics for Language Teachers*. Ann Arbor: University of Michigan Press.

————. 1971. "How to Compare Two Cultures." In *Linguistics Across Cultures*. Ann Arbor: University of Michigan Press.

Lafayette, Robert C. 1988. "Integrating the Teaching of Culture into the Foreign Language Classroom." In *Toward a New Integration of Language and Culture*, edited by Alan J. Singerman. Middlebury, VT: Northeast Conference on the Teaching of Foreign Languages, 47-62.

Lafayette, Robert C., and Renate A. Schulz. 1975. "Evaluating Cultural Learnings." In *The Culture Revolution in Foreign Language Teaching*, edited by Robert C. Lafayette. Lincolnwood, IL: National Textbook Company, 104-18.

Mantle-Bromley, Corinne. 1992. "Preparing Students for Meaningful Culture Learning." *Foreign Language Annals* 25, 2:117-27.

Morain, Genelle. 1976. "Visual Literacy: Reading Signs and Designs in the Foreign Culture." *Foreign Language Annals* 9, 3:210-16.

Moore, Zena T. 1994. "The Portfolio and Testing Culture." In *Teaching, Testing and Assessment: Making the Connection*, edited by Charles R. Hancock. Lincolnwood, IL: National Textbook, 163-82.

Nostrand, Howard L. 1978. "The 'Emergent Model' Applied to Contemporary France." *Contemporary French Civilization* 2, 2:277-94.

Pesola, Carol Ann. 1991. "Culture and the Curriculum in the Elementary School Foreign Language Classroom." *Foreign Language Annals* 24, 4:331-46.

Robinson, Gail L. 1988. *Crosscultural Understanding.* New York: Prentice Hall.

———. 1978. "The Magic-Carpet-Ride-to-Another-Culture Syndrome: An International Perspective." *Foreign Language Annals* 11, 2:135-46.

Savoie, Norman R. 1987. "A French Culture Course for Non-Language Majors." *ADFL Bulletin* 18, 2:55-59.

Scanlan, Timothy M. 1980. "Another Foreign Language Skill: Analyzing Photographs." *Foreign Language Annals* 13, 3:209-13.

Seelye, H. Ned. 1993. *Teaching Culture: Strategies for Intercultural Communication.* Lincolnwood, IL: National Textbook Company.

Shrum, Judith L. and Eileen W. Glisan. 1994. *Teacher's Handbook: Contextualized Language Instruction.* Boston, MA: Heinle and Heinle.

Silber, Ellen, exec. ed. 1992. "Close Encounters of a Literary Kind: Teaching Language in Context." In *Collaborare: News of Academic Alliances in Foreign Languages and Literatures,* School/College Faculty Cooperatives 7 (2 & 3). Tarrytown, NY: Marymount College.

Silber, Ellen, ed. 1991. *Critical Issues in Foreign Language Instruction.* New York and London: Garland Publications.

Singerman, Alan J., ed. 1996. *Acquiring Cross-Cultural Competence: Four Stages for Students of French.* Lincolnwood, IL: National Textbook Company.

Spinelli, Emily. 1985. "Increasing the Functional Culture Content of the Foreign Language Class." In *Meeting the Call for Excellence in the Foreign Language Classroom,* edited by Patricia B. Westphal. Lincolnwood, IL: National Textbook Company, 63-70.

Spinelli, Emily, and H. Jay Siskin. 1992. "Selecting, Presenting and Practicing Vocabulary in a Culturally-Authentic Context." *Foreign Language Annals* 25, 4:305-15.

Stewart, Edward C., and Milton Bennett. 1991. *American Cultural Patterns: A Cross-Cultural Perspective.* Yarmouth, MA: Intercultural Press.

Valette, Rebecca M. 1977. "The Culture Test." In *Modern Language Testing,* 2d ed. New York: Harcourt, Brace, Jovanovich, 263-81.

West, Michael J. and Richard Donato. 1995. "Stories and Stances: Cross-Cultural Encounters with African Folktales." *Foreign Language Annals* 28 (fall).

Wildner-Bassett, Mary E. 1990. "A Video Visit to the Land of Them: Commercials and Culture in the Classroom." *Die Unterrichtspraxis* 23, 1:54-60.

NEW TECHNOLOGIES IN SUPPORT OF FOREIGN LANGUAGES

Bush, Michael D., ed. and Robert M. Terry, assoc. ed. 1997. *Technology-Enhanced Language Learning.* Lincolnwood, IL: National Textbook Company. (The ACTFL Foreign Language Education Series.)

Smith, William Flint, ed. 1989. *Modern Technology in Foreign Language Education: Applications and Projects.* Lincolnwood, IL: National Textbook Company.

ELEMENTARY SCHOOL FOREIGN LANGUAGE PROGRAMS

Curtain, Helena and Carol Ann Bjornstad Pesola. 1994. *Languages and Children: Making the Match, Foreign Language Instruction for an Early Start in Grades K-8.* 2nd ed. White Plains, NY: Longman Publishing Group.

Lipton, Gladys C. 1998. *Practical Handbook to Elementary Foreign Language Programs (FLES*),* 3rd ed. Lincolnwood, IL: National Textbook Company.

―――. 1992. *Elementary Foreign Language Programs (PLES*). An Administrator's Handbook.* Lincolnwood, IL: National Textbook Company.

Met, Miriam, ed. 1998. *Critical Issues in Early Second Language Learning: Building for Our Children's Future*. Glenview, IL: Scott Foresman/Addison Wesley.

Rosenbusch, Marcia H. June 1995. *Guidelines for Starting an Elementary School Foreign Language Program*. (ERIC DIGEST ED383227.)

————. 1995. "Language Learners in the Elementary School: Investing in the Future." In *Foreign Language Learning: The Journey of a Lifetime*, edited by Richard Donato and Robert Terry. Lincolnwood, IL: National Textbook Company.

MIDDLE SCHOOL FOREIGN LANGUAGE PROGRAMS

American Council on the Teaching of Foreign Languages. 1994. *Foreign Language Annals* 27:1 (spring). Special Middle School Edition.

Met, Miriam. 1994. "Foreign Language Instruction in Middle Schools: A New View for the Coming Century." In *Annual Volume of the American Council on the Teaching of Foreign Languages*. Hastings-on-Hudson, NY: American Council on the Teaching of Foreign Languages.

————. February 1996. "Middle Schools and Foreign Languages: A View for the Future." (ERIC DIGEST ED392246.)

North Carolina Department of Public Instruction. 1991. *Building Bridges: A Guide to Second Languages in the Middle Grades*. Raleigh, NC: North Carolina Department of Public Instruction.

Wisconsin Association of Foreign Language Teachers (WAFLT) Task Force on Middle School Foreign Language. 1993. *Foreign Languages at the Middle School Level*. Milwaukee, WI: WAFLT.

ARTICULATION

Byrnes, Heidi. July 1990. "Foreign Language Program Articulation from High School to University." (ERIC DIGEST.)

————. 1990. "Priority: Curriculum Articulation. Addressing Curriculum Articulation in the '90s: A Proposal." *Foreign Language Annals* 23:4, 281-92.

LaFleur, Richard. 1998. *Latin for the 21st Century: From Concept to Classroom*. Reading, MA: Scott Foresman/Addison Wesley/Longman.

New York State Association of Foreign Language Teachers. September 1989. *Language Association Bulletin: A Special Issue on Articulation* XLI, 1. Cortlandt, NY: New York State Association of Foreign Language Teachers.

Wilson, JoAnne. 1988. "Foreign Language Program Articulation: Building Bridges from Elementary to Secondary School." (ERIC DIGEST ED301069.)

Appendix A: Standards for Foreign Language Learning

COMMUNICATION

Communicate in Languages Other Than English

Standard 1.1: Students engage in conversations, provide and obtain information, express feelings and emotions, and exchange opinions.

Standard 1.2: Students understand and interpret written and spoken language on a variety of topics.

Standard 1.3: Students present information, concepts, and ideas to an audience of listeners or readers on a variety of topics.

CULTURES

Gain Knowledge and Understanding of Other Cultures

Standard 2.1: Students demonstrate an understanding of the relationship between the practices and perspectives of the culture studied.

Standard 2.2: Students demonstrate an understanding of the relationship between the products and perspectives of the culture studied.

CONNECTIONS

Connect with Other Disciplines and Acquire Information

Standard 3.1: Students reinforce and further their knowledge of other disciplines through the foreign language.

Standard 3.2: Students acquire information and recognize the distinctive viewpoints that are only available through the foreign language and its cultures.

COMPARISONS

Develop Insight into the Nature of Language and Culture

Standard 4.1: Students demonstrate understanding of the nature of language through comparisons of the language studied and their own.

Standard 4.2: Students demonstrate understanding of the concept of culture through comparisons of the cultures studied and their own.

COMMUNITIES

Participate in Multilingual Communities at Home and Around the World

Standard 5.1: Students use the language both within and beyond the school setting.

Standard 5.2: Students show evidence of becoming life-long learners by using the language for personal enjoyment and enrichment.

APPENDIX B: STUDENT PROMPTS USED IN ARTICULATION AND ACHIEVEMENT PROJECT

WRITTEN ASSESSMENTS

These assessments are valid only when they reflect the instructional program. They can be adapted to any language.

STUDENT #_____   **STAGE I FRENCH**

Directions: Before beginning to write, think about what you want to say. Leave time at the end to look over your work and to make corrections if necessary. You will have 25 minutes to complete this assignment.

Write a postcard to your pen pal in Martinique. Tell him or her that your close friend is going to travel there during the school vacation. Describe your friend. You may want to write about age, appearance, likes, and dislikes. You may also add any information about your friend you think your pen pal will find interesting.

STUDENT #_____   **STAGE II FRENCH**

Directions: Before beginning to write, think about what you want to say in order to write a well-organized letter. Leave time at the end to look over your work and to make corrections if necessary. You will have 30 minutes to complete this assignment.

Write a short letter to your pen pal in Québec or another French-speaking part of Canada. Tell him or her that your close friend is going to travel there during the school vacation. Describe your friend as fully as possible. You may want to write about age, appearance, likes, and dislikes. You make also add any information about your friend you think your pen pal will find interesting.

Directions: Before beginning to write, think about what you want to say in order to write a well-organized letter. Leave time at the end to look over your work and to make corrections if necessary. You will have 40 minutes to complete this assignment.

You have met your ideal friend. Write a journal entry telling in as much detail as possible what the person is like and why you like him or her.

Directions: Before beginning to write, think about what you want to say in order to write a well-organized letter. Leave time at the end to look over your work and to make corrections if necessary. You will have 30 minutes to complete this assignment.

Your friend asks you to write a letter of reference recommending him or her for a position as a camp counselor (conseiller) in Québec for 8- to 10-year-old campers. A good letter of reference usually includes:

- how long you've known the person about whom you are writing;

- a detailed description of the individual's personal qualities, including a particular event that demonstrated one or more of the qualities you have described; and

- reasons why he or she will be a good counselor.

Directions: Before beginning to write, think about what you want to say. Express yourself in a well-organized essay. Leave time at the end to look over your work and to make corrections if necessary. You will have 40 minutes to complete this assignment.

The Value of Friendship

Some people say that friendship is more important than money. Agree or disagree, using examples from your own knowledge or experience.

Oral Assessments

These assessments are valid only when they reflect the instructional program.

Student #_____   **STAGE I** FRENCH

Imagine you are having a phone conversation with a good friend. Tell him or her about a friend you made while visiting France. Describe your new friend with any information that is relevant and interesting. Say as much as you can.

Student #_____   **STAGE II** FRENCH

A good friend is traveling to Paris to learn French, and will be staying with a French family. You have agreed to help him or her by calling the family to make final arrangements. During the conversation, the host parents ask you to tell them a little about your friend. Tell them about his or her likes and dislikes; describe his or her personality. Add any other information you think is important or interesting.

Student #_____   **STAGE III** FRENCH

A French-speaking exchange student has recently enrolled at your school. As a member of the International Club, you want to help this student feel welcome. Knowing that social customs vary from country to country, give some advice and suggestions to this student on making new friends here.

Imagine you are on an exchange trip. After dinner with your host family, the topic of the conversation turns to friendship. Tell a story about an event that changed the nature of your friendship with someone. Talk about what happened to your friendship after this event, for better or for worse.

Summarize the ideas you expressed in your essay on the value of friendship. (Some people say that friendship is more important than money.)

Appendix C: Sample Assessment Activities

Examples of Performance-Based Activities

During the course of the Articulation and Achievement Project, participants from both the secondary and postsecondary levels developed performance-based assessment tasks supporting the Language Learning Continuum. Representative examples of these activities are included in this appendix to provide readers with an understanding of the breadth and depth of this type of assessment. Care should be taken to evaluate student performance at any given stage by reference to the appropriate description of that stage in the Language Learning Continuum.

Many of the activities listed here for a particular stage may be used for any or all of the other stages, as appropriate. The level of student performance, as described in the Language Learning Continuum, becomes the critical factor in determining satisfactory completion of any given assessment activity.

Stage I

Daily and Leisure Activities

- Write a short letter to your pen pal describing your daily activities in school and after school. Also describe what you like to do on weekends or at parties.
- Write entries in a journal describing your activities during each day of the week.
- Read some journal entries of a classmate and tell the class about his or her likes and dislikes.

- Your pen pal is coming to visit you. Write a letter to him or her describing the activities you are planning during his or her stay and asking if he or she likes these various activities.

- Several friends from the target country come to your home to study after school. Introduce them to your family.

- Ask your partner about his or her favorite leisure activity. Record the responses and report your findings to the class.

- You have been given a ticket to the Olympic Games. List all the sporting events you have chosen to attend.

- You are at a friend's house and decide to watch television. Suggest various programs to your friend and tell him or her why you like them.

WEATHER OR SEASONS

- Listen to or read a weather report and present it to the class.

- Your pen pal would like to visit you. Write a letter to him or her describing what the weather is like in your town or city during each month or season of the year.

- You are at the beach, the mountains, or the campground. Write a postcard to your teacher describing the weather where you are and the activities in which you are participating.

HOUSE, HOME, OR FAMILY

- Write a short, simple real estate advertisement describing either the house you are selling or the apartment you would like to rent.

- Make a list of the items you need to furnish each room of your new apartment. Cut pictures from magazines or newspapers that reflect your needs. Make a collage with the pictures and describe your needs to the class, using your collage for illustration.

- Show a photograph of your family to the class and explain who each person is. Then write captions for the photograph in which you describe each person. Send the photograph and captions to your pen pal.

- Describe what you are going to purchase as a birthday gift for each member of your family.

- Videotape a tour of your home in which you show and describe each room.

School and Classroom

- Fill in your daily class schedule on the attached form.
- Write your pen pal describing your school schedule, your teachers, and what you like and dislike about each class.
- Videotape a tour of your classroom in which you describe the academic subject, the teacher, and the relevant objects in the room.
- In a face-to-face conversation, find out about your partner's school schedule and his or her feelings about various school subjects and activities.
- List the contents of your school bag or backpack and explain which class each item is for. Question your partner about the contents of his or her bag or backpack.

Self and Friends

- Write a short letter to your pen pal introducing yourself and telling him or her about yourself.
- Ask your pen pal about himself or herself.
- Prepare a short oral autobiography using props or pictures.
- In small groups, one student at a time will write and say one thing about the person he or she sees in a photograph that is passed from student to student (round-robin).
- In anticipation of an exchange student's arrival, prepare a list of questions to find out as much information as possible about what activities he or she likes and dislikes.

Calendar or Dates

- Fill in the pages of a yearly calendar with months and dates.
- Describe to your partner or write to your pen pal which television programs you watch each day of the week.
- Give the birthdays of your friends and family.
- Survey the students in your class to find out their birthdays. Prepare a graph indicating the number of students born in each month.
- Give the names and dates of holidays that are important to you and your family.
- Make a list of your days off from school and describe what holiday is being celebrated on each date.

- Your partner is ill. Find out what is wrong with him or her by asking questions. Then offer him or her some suggestions on how to get well.

- Listen to a doctor's description of a particular illness and explain what is wrong with the patient.

- You are not feeling well. Write a short note to your friend explaining why you cannot go out with him or her tonight. (This may also be taped as a phone conversation.)

CLOTHING AND SHOPPING

- Fill in a clothing catalog order form with the names of the articles you would like to purchase, the size, color, etc.

- You are working for a large department store. List the items that are available in each department.

- Your pen pal is coming to visit you. He or she will be at your home for a year. Write to him or her describing what articles of clothing he or she will need for each season.

- A friend would like to purchase birthday gifts for various members of your family. Tell him or her what articles of clothing each family member prefers.

- Individually or in pairs, write captions (describing pictured outfits) for photographs to be included in a clothing catalog or fashion magazine.

- With your partner, prepare a dialogue that will be taped. In the dialogue, one role-plays a customer and the other a store clerk. The customer and clerk exchange greetings. The customer then describes the item(s) he or she wishes to buy, and the clerk explains that there are none.

NUMBERS

- Give the scores of various sporting events as the local newspaper is passed around the classroom.

- Using sales circulars from a newspaper, state what prices you must pay for various items.

- Exchange phone numbers with classmates.

- Using a local, foreign, or Minitel phone directory, role-play a tourist calling an information operator to obtain the phone numbers of various restaurants, hotels, banks, etc.

FOOD

- Make a supermarket shopping list for your family for next week.
- In a face-to-face conversation, find out what foods your partner prefers or dislikes for breakfast, lunch, and dinner. Record and report your findings to the class.
- Create a menu for a new restaurant that you and your partner will open next month.
- After reading a recipe, prepare a shopping list. Tell your partner, teacher, or class what supermarkets or small stores you must visit in order to purchase each item on your list.
- Look through the yellow pages in a phone book or advertisements in a newspaper and describe what foods various restaurants specialize in.

TIME

- Write down (using numbers) the arrival and/or departure times of a train or plane as dictated by the teacher or heard in the target language on an audiotape or videotape.
- Using a transportation ticket and working in pairs, question a classmate about the departure and arrival times of trains or planes.
- Read a page from a television guide and tell a classmate what time your favorite programs begin and end.

Stage II

SELF AND OTHERS

- Collect as much information as possible about your partner through questions and discussions, then create a portrait of your partner on newsprint. You may draw and use single words or simple phrases (no full sentences). Make your portrait colorful, perhaps using your partner's favorite colors. Then present your partner to the class via the portrait. (This presentation may be videotaped.)
- Write a short letter to your pen pal, introducing yourself and telling him or her about yourself.
- Videotape or prepare an audiocassette in which you talk briefly about yourself. Exchange the tape with a classmate and provide as much information as possible about the new student whom you see or hear.

- Write a letter to a student attending a school in [target country] that you plan to attend under your school's exchange program. Begin by telling something about yourself. Then inquire about the size of the school, its academic program, its facilities, and the composition of the student body. You may also want to express your concern about your ability to speak the target language in your new environment.

- You will be given several "While You Were Out" forms. Listen carefully to the messages that you find on your answering machine. After you have heard them all, play them back one by one and note the following: the caller's name, his or her phone number, the subject of his or her call. Add a note on any other information you understood.

- A friend is coming to visit you at home, but you need to go out for a short time. Leave a message telling him or her where you are, when you will be back, and how to get in. Your message may be recorded or written.

House and Rooms

Using the real estate advertisements from a magazine or newspaper published in the target language, find lodgings that best suit the needs in two of the following situations. Attach a note of 10 to 12 lines explaining why the selected lodging is optimal in the particular situation.

- You are single, a tennis player, and have no car; or
- Your family includes three children, two parents, a grandmother, and a large dog; or
- You have a new job north of the city and, although you have a car, you would like to ride your bicycle to work; or
- Your parents both have cars, but they leave for work before you must leave for school in the morning. Both you and your parents are runners.

Clothing and Shopping

- Using complete sentences, design a questionnaire to determine respondents' favorite clothes, colors of clothes, brand names, and preferred stores for clothes shopping. The questionnaire may also cover popular accessories. Distribute the surveys to students in another class of the same or higher language ability and analyze their responses.

- With a partner, role-play a dialogue between a salesperson and a customer. The customer wishes to return a particular article of clothing and explains why he or she is not satisfied with it. The salesperson asks questions and may be unwilling to make an exchange.

- With a partner, role-play a dialogue between a parent and his or her son or daughter. The parent is helping him or her buy an article of clothing. However, a conflict arises because their tastes and styles are very different, and they do not agree on price limits.

- With a partner, role-play a dialogue between a customer and a salesperson in the cosmetics department of a well-known department store. The customer is having difficulty deciding how he or she wants to change his or her appearance or simply wants to try something different. The customer and the salesperson have very different tastes.

AUTOMOBILES AND DRIVING

- You are driving down the highway with your wife, husband, or friend to visit your parent, children, or friend when you realize that there is something wrong with the car. A panicky conversation ensues between you and the passenger. Talk about what may be wrong, where you are, and what you should do.

- You are a car salesperson who is trying to sell a car to a customer who knows very little about cars or car prices. The potential buyer has many questions to ask and you have little patience. You are, however, anxious to make the sale.

- You recently bought a new car, but you are having problems with it. You take the car back to the dealer, explain what you think the problem may be, and tell him or her what you think of the car. The dealer attempts to assuage your anger and offer a solution.

GEOGRAPHY AND TRAVEL

- Prepare a one-day diary or journal entry that describes one day of a trip you have taken to a country where the target language is spoken.

- On a world map, locate countries whose principal language is the language you are studying. Also identify bordering countries, indicating their position in relation to each target country, i.e., north, south, east, or west.

- Your family is going on a camping trip. Describe where you are going, what equipment and food you plan to take, what you plan to do upon arrival, and how you feel about taking the trip.
- Write a letter to your cousin in [name of city], in which you tell him or her that you are coming to [the city] to attend a sports event. Ask your cousin if he or she can get you tickets for the event and if you may stay at his or her house. You plan to fly there on July 1 and expect to stay at least one week. Request a written reply from your cousin.
- Write a letter to a hotel manager. Explain that you are planning a trip and that you want some information about the hotel, such as room rates and availability. You may also want to know the location, size, types of rooms, recreational facilities, and points of interest in the area.

Stage III

CAMPUS LIFE AND EDUCATION

- With a visiting exchange student, describe school or campus life in your two countries. Ask for clarification and detail from your partner and be prepared to provide clarification yourself when necessary.
- Write a short essay describing the education system in a country where the target language is spoken. Discuss the similarities to and differences from the education system in your own country.
- Write a short essay describing the ideal high school. Include an introductory paragraph, a description of the building, a description of the course offerings, and a concluding paragraph.
- Write a short essay describing and comparing a secondary school in the target country with your own high school. Conclude your essay with your own opinions about the advantages and disadvantages of each school.

LEISURE ACTIVITIES

- Discuss the vacation customs of families in a country where the target language is spoken.

- Role-play a conversation with your teacher. Discuss the previous summer vacation, the current school year, and plans for the coming months. (This conversation may be videotaped.)
- Write a letter to a pen pal describing your leisure activities and inquiring about those of your pen pal.

DIRECTIONS AND CULTURAL SITES

- Play the role of a city tour guide, describing various buildings, monuments, and other sights in the city being studied.
- Listen to the teacher's description of specific locations of buildings, monuments, and other sights in a specific city or town. Indicate on a diagram supplied by the teacher whether each statement is true or false; if a statement is false, provide the correct information.
- Read in a tourist guidebook about churches and other buildings in a particular city. Guess the meanings of unfamiliar vocabulary items that the teacher has underlined.
- With a partner, imagine yourself in various situations in a town or city, such as getting lost, giving directions to a friend, or asking about buildings or monuments, and discuss these situations.
- Write directions to a particular site on a map. Your partner will read and follow the directions to the indicated site using the same map.
- Write a note to a friend, giving directions to a party.

PUBLIC TRANSPORTATION

- Perform a skit in which the characters are using public transportation in the target country. The skit should demonstrate how to use the particular mode of transportation and also describe some do's and don'ts. (The skit may be videotaped.)
- Listen to directions given by the teacher and follow the directions on your map of a subway, bus, or train system.
- Watch a video segment involving transportation scenes and then answer questions based on the content of the video.
- Read descriptions of subway stations in a city where the target language is spoken. Match the descriptions with visuals provided by the teacher.

- Write a description, based on slides or photographs, of the subway, bus, or train stations in a city. Compare the stations with those with which you are familiar in the United States or other countries.

PERSONAL EXPERIENCES AND INTERESTS

- Listen to a narration of a personal experience. Your teacher will provide you with a list of actions that you will arrange in the correct sequence.
- Read a short story about a personal experience or event and then rewrite the story in your own words.
- With a partner, role-play listening to one another's problems and giving advice.
- Write a letter to an advice column in a target language newspaper or magazine. You may then exchange letters and write responses.
- With a partner, exchange some personal news then respond to it.
- With a partner, write a short note, exchange it, and respond to the note.

FAMOUS PEOPLE

- Pretend to tape a message on a famous person's answering machine, asking several pertinent questions. (The teacher or another student may respond to the questions.)
- Listen to the teacher's description of a famous person and try to figure out who it is.
- Collect some magazine or newspaper articles about famous people and delete their names (using correction fluid). Then trade articles with a classmate and try to figure out who it is.
- Write a letter to a famous person who lives in a country where the target language is spoken. The letter should contain several questions, an expression of what you think about the person and his or her work, and a suggestion about how he or she could improve that work.

Shopping

- Role-play shopping for school items. Describe the things you buy, why you like them, and how much they cost.

- Write and perform a skit about shopping for food in grocery stores in the target country. The skit should include behavior that is culturally appropriate to the situation.

- Watch a video segment on grocery stores in the target country and write short answers to questions based on the content of the video.

- Read a short article about inflation and current prices for various food items in a country where the target language is spoken.

- Write a grocery list, including all the items necessary for a complete dinner for a small group of friends from the target country.

Public Communication Services

- Write and perform a skit that highlights the differences between a post office in the target country and one in the United States.

- With a partner, receive and read detailed instructions for making long-distance phone calls from a post office or pay phone in the target country. Role-play placing a call according to the instructions.

- Read a telegram written on an authentic form from the target country.

Current Events and Issues

- Read an article from a current magazine or newspaper or watch a videotape about a current issue or topic that you are studying. Then take a true or false or multiple-choice quiz that highlights the important ideas about the issue or topic.

- Prepare a taped monologue in which you briefly explain a current issue and state your opinion about it.

- Watch a television news broadcast about a current issue and summarize the opinion presented.

- Read and summarize the main opinions presented in a short editorial in a target-language newspaper.

- Write a short editorial expressing your opinion on a current issue.

Stage IV

CONTEMPORARY ISSUES

- After viewing a film or reading a text focusing on a contemporary issue, write a letter from the point of view of one of the characters in the film or text.
- Write a film review or with partners present an oral review of a contemporary film in the target language.
- Write and perform an original dialogue based on two characters from a film or text.
- Write an advertisement about something you don't want young people to do or suffer from, such as drug use or HIV.
- Compare and contrast American and [another country's] perspectives on the benefits of a major economic agreement such as NAFTA.

CONTEMPORARY LIFE

- Agree or disagree with the following statement: *Computers make life harder.* Use personal experiences to support your opinion.
- With three or four classmates, debate the issue of whether family life is more or less important in today's world; use examples from the news to support your opinion.
- Interview a classmate to find out his or her opinion on a current topic of social importance, for example the impact of musical icons such as Madonna on young people, the necessity of bilingual education, English as an official language, or the concept of teaching children at home instead of at school. After ascertaining the reasons for your classmate's opinion, agree or disagree and explain your own stance.
- Compare and contrast traditional medicine with alternative medicine. State the advantages and disadvantages of each approach.
- Agree or disagree with the following statement: **Zoos are unethical.** Give reasons to support your opinion.

- Write an autobiography highlighting the events of your life. Include three people who have influenced your life and the reasons for their influence.
- Narrate an accident that you have experienced or witnessed.
- Describe in detail an embarrassing situation that you have experienced.
- Role-play your candidacy in a race for election to the Student Council. Describe yourself as a person and as a candidate and explain why you should be elected.
- Choose one adjective that best describes your personality and then relate an anecdote that illustrates this facet.
- Write an essay explaining what you would like to do after graduation and explain the reasons for your choice.

TRAVEL AND LEISURE

- With a partner, describe a place in the target country in one of the following ways: role-play a customer and travel agent exchange or try to convince two other classmates to visit a chosen vacation site.

SCHOOL AND CAMPUS LIFE

- Explain to an incoming freshman how to survive at your school or college.

Stage V

CONTEMPORARY ISSUES

- Watch a video on a country where the target language is spoken. Then write a letter to a friend giving general information about that country.
- Write a letter to your teacher expressing your opinion about a topic or issue that you have studied in language class. Offer your advice and suggestions for improving the course.
- Summarize a class discussion on recognizing and preventing racism in the school and in the community.

- Write to a pen pal in another country, detailing your understanding of the political events in that country based on what you have read or seen in the media or heard from native speakers.
- After studying the events of a recent trial and judgment, debate with your classmates the legitimacy of capital punishment.

CULTURE AND HISTORY

- As the teacher describes the scene in a well-known painting, draw the scene as you visualize it from the description. (This activity may be accompanied by music of the same historical period.)
- Research, in the target language, the life and work of a famous painter or musician. You become the artist or musician as you present "his" or "her" life, artistic or musical style, and technique to the class. Then compare your effort with that of other students.
- Take notes on a lecture given by your teacher or a classmate about an artist or composer. Then select a work of the artist or composer and critique it in an essay, referring to the notes you took on subject matter and technique.
- Plan a guided tour to a museum in the target country where you will view artworks from two historical periods. Then write a summary of the two periods and describe one representative artist from each. Compare and contrast both the periods and the artists.
- Imagine yourself as a nineteenth-century artist, musician, or scientist. Prepare a convincing defense of your artistic, musical, or scientific style to persuade the academicians to accept your work. (This performance may be videotaped.)
- Paint an animal of your choice in the style of an artist studied during the year. Then write an essay on your work, explaining the style.
- Role-play a film director whose recent release was so successful that the public is demanding another film. Choose one of the films viewed during the year and write or discuss an outline for the plot of a sequel.

LITERARY TEXTS

- After listening to classmates' presentations on several poems, compare and contrast the subject and technique in three of them.

- Write a summary of your class notes on one of the literary works studied during the year. The summary should include character portraits, action or plot, style, etc.
- Identify the following passages from works read during the year and place the passages in the context of the work, describing characters and action. (The teacher will provide the passages.)
- After reading a particular text, creatively interpret a character, event, or scene, using your personal talents and interests in music, drawing, costume design, dance, etc.
- Write and recite a poem or a short passage in the style of an author studied during the year.

School

- Convince a classmate that a long sequence of foreign language study is essential for students in elementary and secondary school to develop communicative competency in a language.
- Using content from a project in another class (science, math, social studies), design a lesson in which you teach your language class about the project. Use the appropriate vocabulary and make a sketch or present the project itself. Give a step-by-step explanation and describe what you learned from the project.
- Conduct a survey of your classmates to determine their views on a particular school policy (absences, homework, smoking, hats). Write a report on your findings and present it to the class.

Personal Needs

- Send a letter to a catalog company from which you have received an item of clothing that does not fit. Explain the problem and negotiate the terms of returning the item.
- A doctor has prescribed medication for your illness, but you are having an adverse reaction to it. Call the doctor to describe your symptoms and request further treatment.
- After promising a friend that you will accompany him or her to a holiday dance or celebration, you have been offered a complimentary flight to New York City for the weekend. Your friend, however, is counting on you. Call the friend to explain the complicated circumstances.

APPENDIX D: SAMPLE PORTFOLIO TEMPLATES

The templates included here reflect activities that require students to use a variety of modalities and higher order thinking skills to complete the assignment. The activities may take several weeks to complete and can be evaluated separately or as a whole. In any case, student performance should be regarded as progress toward achievement of stage goals.

STAGE I

1. Use your language skills in the community. For example, start a correspondence in the foreign language with residents of a local nursing home, or volunteer to work with a social service agency that provides services to community members whose first language is not English.

2. Introduce yourself to another person via a short letter, postcard, or e-mail message. Request information (likes, dislikes, food, school) and report your findings to your classmates.

3. Listen to a commercial in the foreign language. Write a brief description of the product or service. Then create an audio or video broadcast of a product or service of your choice.

4. Design and write a children's book using vocabulary on related topics (pets or other animals, transportation, shopping). For example, create a touch-and-feel book of zoo or domestic animals. Make an audio recording of the book's script. Read the finished product to classes at a local elementary school.

STAGE II

1. Write a letter to a student at a school in the country where the target language is spoken to inform him or her that you plan to attend under your school's exchange program. First, give information about yourself (your age, your family, your interests). Then, inquire about the size of the school, its academic program, its facilities, and the composition of the student body.

2. Prepare a survey on the likes and dislikes of your classmates. Choose the topics yourself (foods, sports, holidays, school, and any other information you wish). Develop at least 10 questions and then interview your classmates. Report your survey findings to the class in a well-prepared presentation, which will be videotaped.

STAGE III

You are reviewing the lives and works of six important **visual artists*** whom you have studied.

1. You see before you **four paintings** by four different **artists.** Your teacher will read a description in the foreign language of each of the **artists who painted the pictures.** As you listen, you must correctly identify each **artist and his or her corresponding painting.**

2. You read an interview with a famous creative person in a foreign language magazine or newspaper. List the kinds of questions asked in the interview, and then find and underline the key answers in the text. In English or the foreign language (depending on whether a teacher wishes to assess reading skills alone or in combination with writing skills), comment in writing on one or two major issues that you learned about from reading the interview.

3. Select a partner and, as a pair, assume the roles of a famous **artist** and a journalist. The journalist, somewhat familiar with the **artist's** life and work, asks questions in the foreign language that are designed to reveal to the listening audience (a) key events in the **artist's** life, (b) the **artist's favorite work** with reasons for the choice, and (c) the **artist's** plans for the future.

4. Write a letter to your favorite **artist.** Express your opinions about the **artist** and his or her work. Also state the **feelings or emotions that the artist's work** evokes in you.

*Depending on the foreign language curriculum, a teacher may choose to replace "visual artists" and the accompanying text with another typical and/or timely category related to the content of Stage III, such as musicians, historians, or scientists.

STAGE IV

Having studied the **NAFTA** issue and having listened to representatives of the **AFL-CIO** and the **Mexican ambassador** comment on the topic of **NAFTA**,* complete the following:

1. In the foreign language, write an essay in which you compare and contrast the two points of view. In your essay also state your position on this issue and explain the reasons for your choice.

2. In the foreign language, debate with your peers the advantages and disadvantages of **NAFTA**, using arguments set forth in your essay.

*Depending on the foreign language curriculum and current world events, a teacher may choose to replace "NAFTA" and the accompanying text with another issue related to the content of Stage IV, such as the Free Trade Agreement, immigration in France, or the reunification of Germany.

STAGE V *

1. Write a letter in **French to Michel de Montaigne** in which you analyze his ideas on **education** from his essay **"L'Education des Enfants."** Offer your opinion of these ideas as they relate to contemporary **educational practices.**

2. You are a **nineteenth-century French artist** who wishes to be accepted to the **Art Academy. In French,** prepare a convincing defense of your **artistic style** to persuade **academicians** to accept your candidacy. Videotape your defense.

3. Should a liberal arts college or a university require students to study a foreign language? In the foreign language, state your point of view, explain your reasons, and support your opinion based on discussions in class. Write a letter to a college or university language department expressing your ideas.

---

*Depending on the foreign language curriculum, a teacher may choose to replace the specific topic with another topic related to the content of Stage V.

Appendix E: Student Assessment Results

Articulation and Achievement Project

The data on these pages reflect the results of oral and written performance assessments produced by middle school, high school, and college students throughout New England from 1993 to 1994.

The prompts used in these assessments can be found in Appendix B. Students' written and taped responses were evaluated using the rubrics on page 102.

French Written Assessments
Articulation and Achievement Project
Fall 1993 and Spring 1994

STAGE I		=	279
6	rec'd 0	=	2.15%
118	rec'd 1	=	42.29%
143	rec'd 2	=	51.26%
12	rec'd 3	=	4.30%
STAGE II		=	148
1	rec'd 0	=	0.68%
37	rec'd 1	=	25.00%
92	rec'd 2	=	62.16%
18	rec'd 3	=	12.16%
STAGE III		=	103
1	rec'd 0	=	0.97%
23	rec'd 1	=	22.33%
65	rec'd 2	=	63.11%
14	rec'd 3	=	13.59%

STAGE IV		=	130
48	rec'd 1	=	36.92%
66	rec'd 2	=	50.77%
16	rec'd 3	=	12.31%
STAGE V		=	77
42	rec'd 1	=	54.50%
33	rec'd 2	=	42.80%
2	rec'd 3	=	2.70%

TOTAL STUDENTS RATED 737

FRENCH ORAL ASSESSMENTS

Articulation and Achievement Project
Fall 1993 and Spring 1994

STAGE I		=	208
12	rec'd 0	=	5.77%
84	rec'd 1	=	40.38%
103	rec'd 2	=	49.52%
9	rec'd 3	=	4.33%
STAGE II		=	185
1	rec'd 0	=	0.54%
77	rec'd 1	=	41.62%
93	rec'd 2	=	50.27%
14	rec'd 3	=	7.57%
STAGE III		=	124
2	rec'd 0	=	1.61%
44	rec'd 1	=	35.48%
66	rec'd 2	=	53.23%
12	rec'd 3	=	9.68%
STAGE IV		=	66
34	rec'd 1	=	51.52%
24	rec'd 2	=	36.36%
8	rec'd 3	=	12.12%

STAGE V		=	49
12	rec'd 1	=	24.49%
30	rec'd 2	=	61.22%
7	rec'd 3	=	14.29%

TOTAL STUDENTS RATED 632

Spanish Written Assessments

Articulation and Achievement Project
Fall 1993 and Spring 1994

STAGE I		=	282
35	rec'd 0	=	12.41%
130	rec'd 1	=	46.10%
99	rec'd 2	=	35.11%
18	rec'd 3	=	6.38%

STAGE II		=	146
1	rec'd 0	=	0.68%
39	rec'd 1	=	26.71%
78	rec'd 2	=	53.43%
28	rec'd 3	=	19.18%

STAGE III		=	113
1	rec'd 0	=	0.89%
45	rec'd 1	=	39.82%
53	rec'd 2	=	46.90%
14	rec'd 3	=	12.39%

STAGE IV		=	68
35	rec'd 1	=	51.47%
14	rec'd 2	=	20.59%
19	rec'd 3	=	27.94%

STAGE V		=	41
22	rec'd 1	=	53.66%
12	rec'd 2	=	29.27%
7	rec'd 3	=	17.07%

TOTAL STUDENTS RATED 650

SPANISH ORAL ASSESSMENTS

Articulation and Achievement Project
Fall 1993 and Spring 1994

STAGE I		=	186
11	rec'd 0	=	5.91%
57	rec'd 1	=	30.65%
92	rec'd 2	=	49.46%
26	rec'd 3	=	13.98%
STAGE II		=	123
60	rec'd 1	=	48.78%
55	rec'd 2	=	44.72%
8	rec'd 3	=	6.50%
STAGE III		=	59
1	rec'd 0	=	1.69%
35	rec'd 1	=	59.32%
18	rec'd 2	=	30.51%
5	rec'd 3	=	8.48%
STAGE IV		=	86
3	rec'd 0	=	3.48%
52	rec'd 1	=	60.47%
24	rec'd 2	=	27.91%
7	rec'd 3	=	8.14%
STAGE V		=	20
12	rec'd 1	=	60.00%
6	rec'd 2	=	30.00%
2	rec'd 3	=	10.00%

TOTAL STUDENTS RATED 474

APPENDIX F: SAMPLE STUDENT WRITINGS

WRITING SAMPLES

The following pages contain actual student writing samples collected during the course of the Articulation and Achievement Project. They are organized by Stage, I through V. The stage designation for each of these samples refers to the fact that the students who wrote the samples were enrolled in classes that had performance expectations equivalent to the stage indicated. The actual work represented here may fall below the expectation for the stage, may meet it, or exceed it. The age range spans from 12 to 20 years. The background and experience of each student is equally varied.

The samples have been included here to provide you with the opportunity to evaluate them, to discuss them, to share ideas with colleagues about recommendations you might make to these students regarding their work, etc. We hope that you will find using these samples in conjunction with the rubrics found on page 102 a stimulating and interesting experience.

Note: In a few cases, because the student work was in some way representative but not legible, the sample has been typed exactly as written or has been darkened for printing.

Stage I

Hola, Mí amiga es Vivianna. Vivianna es muy guapa.
Ella es morena y muy intellegarte Ella es muy divertida
y muy buen en deportes. Ella come ensalada, pan,
carne y pescado. Viviana va a una sinagoga.
Ella es un pinor. Ella muy afisinosdo fótbal
tenisysoft bál. Ella espera en la estación de
ferrocarrill por tú Ella es va tren. Ella lleva
un vestido, zapotos y falda. Ella va a Massachusetts.
Ella es eschua discos hora. Mí escribe carta a
tú porque mí amiga es va a Puerto Rico. Mí
enclosed un fotograf de mí amiga.
                    Carmen

Stage 1

Querido Ana,
    ¿Como estás? Mi amiga vaando
a visitar Puerto Rico. Ella visitando en
la vacaciónes de la escuela en abril.
Ella se llama Pilar. Pilar tiene quince
años. Pilar es morena. Ella tiene dos
hermanas y tres hermanos. Te gustan
los deportes. Te gusta nadando mucho.
Te gusta escuchar la radio tambien.
No te gusta ayudar en casa
No te gusta lavar la ropa o
lavar los carros tambien. Ella
es muy divertido. Pilar es
inteligente tambien. Pilar es alta. Está
muy contenta.
               ¡Adios!
Stage I   -Manuela

Nombre,

Hola. ¿Como Está? Yo escribe tú
por mi amigo Monica. Ella is sale
por Puerto Rico de vacaciones Ella es
muy bonita y simpatica. Ella es rubia
and alta. Monica guesta practica
el Fútbol, el softbal y el besquitbol.
Ella es muy integente. Ella toma
un tren Puerto Rico un vernes. Ella es
cimplir trece años en Sempiembe. Ella
guesta come tocos.

Juanita

Stage 1

Stage 1 French

Chere Chail,

Bonjour! Ça Va? Ça va bein. Mon ami, Lester, est visite de Martinique. Il est peti, brun,

Sincerly,
Jeremy

Stage 1

Chère John

      Ma amie visite Martinique.
Elle est petite et Blonde. Elle est très
sympa. Elle est très comique et très
populaire. Elle a deux sac. Elle parlaire
beaucoup. Elle a seize ans. Elle deteste le
football. Elle adore le volley. Elle aime
parler au telephone. Elle est très
interessant et très entelligente.

              ta copine
              Lorraine

Stage I

Querido amigo:

Mi amigo va a trabajar a Puerto Rico este verano. Se llama Jeff. Es bajo. Tiene pelo corto y color cafe. Tiene viente años. Se gusta comida mucho! Es muy inteligent y se gusta escuchar musica rock. Es muy loco pero divertido.

Adios
Tom

Chère Florence,

Ça va? Je suis contente que l'année de l'école est fini. C'était difficile! Je prenais six cours: français, anglais, histoire/geographie, maths, biologie et chinois. J'avais beaucoup de devoirs! J'aimais ma classe de biologie. Mon prof était sympa et la classe était intéressante. Je n'aimais pas maths. Je pense que c'était trop difficile pour moi. Histoire/geographie, c'était pas difficile, mais un peu ennuyeuse. Anglais était amusant, je pense que j'apprenais beaucoup.

Ma famille est bon. Maman et Papa iront en Chine pendant l'été. Irene ira au colonie de vacances. Andy, aussi, ira au colonie de vacance pour chinois. J'irai au colonie de vacance pour l'escrime. J'irai aussi en Californie pour un tournois de l'escrime.

Je faisais beaucoup de l'escrime cette année. Je pratique deux ou trois fois par semaine. Je faisais aussi du surf de neige. J'adore ça! Je suis allée à Sunday River avec une copine. Pendant les vacances de Fevrier, ma famille et moi, nous sommes allés au Vermont pour faire du ski et surf de neige. C'était un hiver très froid. Maintenant, il fait chaud et il fait du soleil. Aujourd'hui, c'est presque 90°! Quelle est la température en France? Je ne peux pas attendre pour ma visite, à Lyon!

Quand je suis à Lyon, il y a beacoup de choses que je veux faire. Je voudrais aller au parc de la Tête d'Or, où nous promenerons. Je voudrais aller aussi au Miribel Jonage! J'apprendrais faire de la planche à voile.

La derniere fois j'étais à Lyon, nous sommes allés à la plage de la Mediterranée. Est-ce que nous pouvons aller encore? Nous apporteron nos maillots de bain et nous ferons de la natation dans la mer! Je voudrais aussi faire du shopping dans la quartier piétonnier, où il y a beaucoup de petites boutiques! Et bien sur, je n'oublie pas l'histoire de Lyon. Nous irons à la cathédrale de Saint-Jean, et la place Bellecour, avec la statue du roi Louis XIV!

Grosses Bises,

Paulette

Accueil Pierre,

Ça va ? Oui, ça va. Je suis ~~content~~ t'écrire parce que mon petit-ami est allé a Paris la deuxieme semaine de Juin pour son vacances. Il veux voir la Tour Eiffel et la Louvre. Peux-tu aider mon ami voir tous les choses a Paris ?

Il aime promener et aussi il est un bon danser. Il prends des classes avec moi à la studio. Il a des yeux brun et des cheveaux brun, aussi. Il a 5'10" et il a un bon structure. Il a vingt ans, son anniversaire est en juillet, jusque comme toi. Quelle coincidence ! Non ?

Il n'aime pas des personnes qui pense que ils ont magnifique parce que ils ont ennuyeux, aussi, il n'aime pas des enfants. Je ne sais pas pourquoi mais ça c'est une probleme de notre relationship! C'est la vie.

S'il vous plait, ecrire-moi et dire dit-moi ton numero de telephone pour lui! Je veux que je suis allé a Paris ~~pour~~ donq nous peuvons attendre.

amies toujours,
Jeanne

Chère Kate,

Bonjour mon amie! J'ai besoin t'ecrivez un lettre, parce nous ne parle pas en deux annees J'ai un amie, Phoebe. Elle est tres magnifique. Elle fait du Basket, et football. Elle est tres intelligent. J'aime Phoebe. J'ai un petit amie, Frank, mais il est laide et il n'est pas intelligent. Je joues du basket apres l'ecole en lundi, mercredi et jeudi avec mon amie Mellissa. Mellissa est excellent!

A l'ecole ma courses; tres dificle. En science, mon prof n'aime pas moi, mais je n'aime lui. L'histoire c'est chouette. Mon prof, M.   est tres bom.

A ma maison, j'ai laver la voiture et le besein le mange le chien. Ma soeur besion le fait du shopping.

En dimanche, Je vais aller au cinema, et je vais fait du shopping. Je suis un depensiere. J'aime le shopping. Je fait du shopping avec Phoebe, Mellissa et Anna. Anna as un petit amie. Il s'appelle Nick. Elle est alleé l'ecole boarding pour lui paren. J'ai mal au docteur. J'ai besion le medicin.

Amitiés,
Maria

Hola Mercedes,   nueve de mayo.
        Como tienes tu? Yo es muy bien. mi
amiga Isabel, esta mexico en vacationes. Ella
esta de los Estados Unidos   y tiene hablo
español dos años. Ella tiene no morena
haic y es muy pequeño. Isabel tiene viente
menos tres años. Su cupleano es viente y
ocho de Enero. Ella es muy importante mi
y es no fee. Ella tiene dos hermanos y no
hermanae. Isabel tiene no novio pero mucho
amigos. Hasta leɥego.

Stage II

Querida Margarita,
 ¿Cómo estás? Esta carta es para decirte
que una gran amiga mía va a visitar a México.
Mi amiga se llama _____, y tiene catorce años.
Ella vive en la ciudad de Boston con su mamá
y su hermanita. Sara es rubia y es baja. A
ella le gusta el color verde porque tiene ojos
verdes. A ella le gusta bailar y cantar. Es una
gran amiga y te encantaría su compañía.
 Ella va a llegar a las 6:00 PM. en el
avión que sale a las 3:00 P.M. de Boston. Ella
te va a esperar en la avenida del pueblo.
La encontrarás detrás de la fuente. Te encantará
su amistad y vas a gozar mucho. Que gozes!
                              Tu Amiga,
                              Louisa

Hola Juan,

¿Que tal? Yo estoy muy bien aquí en Boston. Mi amigo Pablo iba a México durante nos vacaciones de marzo. ¿Tú conocía Pablo, no? Él esta alto y muy delgado. y tiene pelo negro. Se gusta jugar al tenis y correr. ¿Tú conocía ahora, no? Pablo tiene un trabaja en el hospital de Guatelahara. Él es un estudiante de medicina excelente. Durante la vacacione el trabajando con patientes en el hospital. Debo Tú y Pablo ir a la playa cuando él visite México. ¡Pablo es un persona fantastico!

¡Adios Juan!

⟨Tú amigo Miguel⟩

P.d. ¿ Porque tú no escribes unas cartas por me?

Stage III

Mi amiga ideal se llama Elizabeth. Ella
vivía en Boston, sed ~~se~~ movió a Connecticut
cuando teníamos diez años. Le encontré cuando
teníamos cinco años.

Elizabeth es muy simpática y ~~~~ divertida.
~~~~ Ella tiene el pelo moreno y los ojos verdes.
Ella es muy alta. Elizabeth me visita ~~~~ ^{a menudo}
en Boston y ~~~~ le visito en Connecticut. Vamos
a ~~la~~ Canadá ~~~~ todas los veranos por dos
meses. Somos ~~las~~ amigas mejores. ~~~~
Me llama en el telephono a menudo y le llamo
en el telephono a menudo, tambien. Llamaré a
Elizabeth a noche.

Stage III

    Mi amiga se llama Elizabeth. Elizabeth es muy interesante y muy cómica. Ella vive en una casa cerca de mi casa. Elizabeth asiste a la escuela de Boston Latin y esta en muchas clases conmigo. Ella es muy intelligente y tiene buenas notas. Le ayudo en Matemática y me ayude en Latina. Deseo que ella rea mi hermana.

    Elizabeth ~~venia~~ vino a Boston cuando ~~Elizabeth venia~~ teniamos diez años. Mi madre trabajabas con su madre. Elizabeth y yo encontramos cuando teniamos once años.

    Elizabeth es muy divertida y amo estar con ella. Cuando ~~no~~ vamos a ir a colegio, escribiré unas cartar a ella.

Stage III

Mon meilleur amie est intelligent, droll, et très sympa. Elle est petite avec cheveux blonde. Elle a une figure belle. Mon amie aime faire beaucoup des choses, pour example, les sports, et las activities avec les autre jeunes comme les boums et les dances. Elle adore tous la musique aussi. Elle m'ecoute, et me donne les conseils quand j'ai une problem Si je suis triste, mon amie me fais contente encore. Elle est fantastique.

M. le directeur de l'échange,

    Vous m'avez demandé de vous donner quelques opinions et réactions que j'ai eu à mon visite à Paris. Donc, voici ma réponse.

    En général, j'aimais bien Paris. C'est la capitale de la France et il y a beaucoup de choses qui s'y passent. Mais à mon avis, on y a passé trop de temps. Chaque touriste qui vient à la France peut aller à Paris voir les musées, le Tour Eiffel, les parcs, et les magasins comme nous avon fait - main nous ne comme pas touristes! Nous avons une chance que les touristes n'ont pas - le chance de rester avec les familles française, voir les écoles et les vies des français. Moi, je pence qu'il faut en profiter et passer plus de temps avec les familles. Comme ça, nous purrions comprendre un peu plus comment tout aux écoles marche, voir plus d'etudiants nous pourrions nous adapter plus à la vrai culture [d'une région, oui] de la France. D'ailleurs, c'est plus interessante de faire

(cont)

la conaissance des personnes ave qui
nous restons que de voir beaucoup
d'étrangers!

Aussi, je pense qu'on a essayé de trop
faire. Ça fait mal aux pieds de marcher
d'une musée à une autre toute la journée
Et on n'apprécie pas autant qu'on peut si
on voit des monuments après des monumen
après des mussées après de magasins...
c'est fatigant! Si on essayait de voir un
peu moins et d'avoir un peu plus de
temps à voir les choses qu'on voit et de
temps libre pour s'assecoir on apprécirait
beaucoup plus et on s'amuserait plus
aussi. Une idée est qu'on peut visiter les magasins un matin, puis on peut manger le déjeuner
à un parc, et pour finir le jour on peut visiter
le louvre et puis un restaurant. Pas trop, mais
assez.

J'ai pensé aussi que ça serait amusant
et informatif si on avait nos 'hosts' avec nous
à Paris - ça nous donnera plus de temps à
faire leurs conaissances. on aura des autres
jeunes avec nous (qui seront français!)...

(cont)

tout serait mieux. Peut-être qu'ils ne sauront plus que nous à propos de Paris; mais si c'est la situation. On peut enseigner à tout le monde et voir les réactions, du même temps des américains et des français.

En tout cas, je pense qu'il faut passer moins de temps à Paris, et qu'il faut passer le temps que nous passons, là avec nos français. Et il ne faut pas voir/visiter tant de musées!!

(end)

Stage 4

le 4 mai

Monsieur/Madame

Je m'appelle Hélène Dupuis et je vous écris de vous recommender mon amie comme conseiller de votre camp en Québec. Mon amie s'appelle Marie Moreau et elle a dix-huit ans. Je la connaissais pendant cinq ans. Elle est très fort avec les enfants. Elle vient d'une grande famille tellement elle sait les enfants. Elle a aidé sa mère avec l'autre enfants cadettes dans sa famille.

Marie est très hônet est responsable. Elle est gnereuse et elle aime s'amuser, surtout avec les enfants. Ses parents sont divorcée et tout les enfants vivent avec la mère. Beaucoup de temps, la mère travail et Marie garde les enfants jusqu'à sa mèn revient. J'espère que vous considerez Marie pour ce position. Vous irez la trouver formidable.

Je vous prie l'expression de mes sentiments distingues.

Hélène

Stage IV

Mon ami veux devoir un conseiller à un camp pour les garçons et les filles qui ont neuf ans quand je devrai une grande personne. Robert m'a dit ça quand nous avions six ans. Devenant un conseiller du camp, c'est le but de Robert dans sa vie. Si il ne devra pas un conseiller, j'ai peur que Robert se suicidera. Robert est un peu trop serieux au sujet de son but mais je pense qu'il a la personalité d'être un conseiller magnifique.

Robert est très responsable. Il oublie ~~une~~ toujours toutes ses responsabilités. Tous les jours il se réveille, il mange et il dorme. Il connait toujours ce qu'il faut faire. Il adore les enfants especiallement ceux qui ont neuf ans. Je ne sais pourquoi il les adore mais il ferait tous les possibles pour gagner le sourire d'un enfant.

Robert est aussi un grand homme. Si il y'a quelque chose que les enfant détestent, il détruisont la chose complètement. Il est vraiment une bonne personne qui va devoir un bon conseilles.

Cher Monsieur hego,

Bonjour, j'écrit cet lettre pour mon amie Cheryl. Nous sommes de Montreal et je la savait depuis quinze ans. Elle est très responsable et aussi, elle est magnifique avec les enfants. Elle fait du baby-sitting pour mon frère Seth, qui est neuf ans. Chaque fois qu'elle va à mon maison, Seth crie avec joie: "Cheryl, bonjour! Comment vas-tu?" Il l'aime beaucoup. Elle est symathique mais elle est responsable. Elle est vraiment honête et fait de bon travail tout le temps. Elle a un air formidable et chaque presonne qui faisait sa connaissance l'adore. Je pense que Cheryl soit le meilleure conseiller de tout la colonie de vacances.

Stage 4

Querido Señor,

Yo pienso que mi amiga, MARIA, sería una buena asistente. La tiene saber para ocho años. Ella es símpatica y alegía. Tiene mucha talenta con cabellos. Ella es optimista y inteligente. Se cuida para niños y jovenes. Hace muchas cosas. Juega tenis y fútbol. Nada muy bien y esquia de aquatico. Ella lleva a tiempo siempre y hace sus responsidades. Dice la verdad siempre. Ella sería una buena asistente porque es buenas con personas. Tengo trusta en ella.

Juanita

Stage 4

Señor / Señora:

    Pienso que necesita mi amiga Brigitte. La tengo que conocer por tres años. ^A Ella le encantan los niños. También, a ella le gustan muchos deportes como fútbol americano, basquetbol, y tenis.

    A nuestra universidad ella trabaja a La Escuela de Niños. Ella ayuda los niños comer, beber, y jugar los deportes. También ella enseña los niños en matemáticas y inglés.

    Ella habla español muy bien. Por eso ella puede trabajar con los niños en Costa Rica. Piensa que sea divertido trabajar con niños en una otra país.

    Ella es muy simpática y inteligente. A Los niños les encantaría esta mujer. Ella sería una buena asistente.

Yo hay conocido este persona, Claudia, por cinco años.
Nos encontremos en la escuela secondaria. Claudia haya
trabajndo con mi en un restaurante mexicana y en
un programa de verano en Tejas. Claudia ama
niños pequeños mucho. Claudia tiene mucha paciencia
con niños. Ella quiere trabajar con niños despues de
graduarse de el colegio. Ella quiere ser una
doctora de niños, una pediatriciana, pero tiene muchas
problemas con el clase de quimica. Claudia trabaja
mucho y completa trabajo dificil con no problemas.
Pienso que Claudia seria una doctora buena, porque
ella es muy cariñosa. Claudia escuche de las
problemas de otra personas, tambien. Cuando yo
tengo problemas, conozco puede hablar a Claudia.
Si Claudia decide a no asista escula medica, creo
que ella seria la maestra perfecta. Es la
creencia de mi que Claudia seria una asidente buena.
Claudia es muy atletica, tambien. Ella podria
podria ayudar niños con los actividades atleticcs
como nadar, montar los caballos y jiggu tenis.
Claudia enseñé a mi nadar Claudia ayuda mis
hermanos con los deportes y la seguridad de los
deportes.

STAGE V FRENCH

The Value of Friendship

Sans doute, l'amitié est plus important que l'argent! Bien sur, l'argent est tres important pour les choses matériaux, mais l'amitié est une chose profonde eternelle, et precieuse.

Je n'ai jamais pensé que l'argent est un symbol d'affluence, de pouvoir et de la richesse. Ce n'est pas un symbol d'amour, de compassion, des sentiments, ou de la cour. L'amitié est un symbol de ces choses. Elle represent un rapport fort entre deux personnes. Si l'amitié entre deux personnes marchent, c'est meilleur que tout l'argent du monde.

J'ai beaucoup d'amis. J'espère que je pourrai avoir toujours des amis mais si il n'y aura pas beaucoup d'argent à l'avenir - ce ne sera pas une grande probleme. Etre contente, avoir les rapports avec la famille et les amis...c'est important!

Je suis contente a cause de mes succes, ma famille, mes activités, et mes amis. Pas mon argent. Si, il c'est amusant pour acheter des vetements on la musique quelquefois, mais c'est tout. L'argent ne joue pas une grande role dans ma vie.

Je pense quil est stupide que ~~l'argent~~ beaucoup d'argent est nécessaire pour l'education et les médicaments, etc. Pour recevoir une bonne education, on a besoin d'argent. Alors, l'argent est important pour accomplir des buts.

En conclusion, on peut dire que l'argent est une chose qui ne changera jamais. Il est tres secure. Mais l'amitié est plus precieuse; elle continuera a changer toujours. Nous apprendons de l'amitié. Nous gagnons un grand comprension des personnes et nos differences. L'amitie nous aide à vivre, pleurer, aime, et s'amuser.

L'amité est tellement speciale à moi. J'adore mes amis comme ils sont famille. L'amité est plus important de l'argent parce qu'ils sont ici pour éternité. On parle de tous, et nous partageons nos emotions. Ils sont toujours là quand je veut bien parler à quelqu'un. Ils m'aident quand j'ai des problémes, et j'éspère que je ne les jamais perdre. Maintenant, les amis de l'universite sont vraiement important. Après lycée, il n'y a toujours pas des parents alors il faut qu'on fasse des amis. Au debut c'etait difficile, mais maintenant, apres seuleme: neuf mois, je ne peut pas imaginer ma vie sans eux. Déja, nous avons passé les temps drôle, mauvais, serieux, et triste. Les choses que je me souviens sont les bonnes temps. Nous avons bien amusé, et je suis très comfortable avec eux.

    La gentilesse d'une amie est precieuse. J'ador: d'être ensemble pour parler, jouer, faire des exercises, etudier - n'aporter quoi! On peut avoir les conversations serieuse pour deux ou trois heures. Et, aprés, avec les mêmes amis, on peut jouer du football americaine, ou marcher.

    Personellement, je crois que l'amité est toujours plus important que la monaie. Je choisirais d'accompagne: mes amis toujours. On s'amuse facilement et c'est pour tout ces raisons pour quoi j'adore mes amis avec tout mon coeur.

STAGE V SPANISH
The Value of Friendship

Creo que amistades son mas importantes que el dinero. Amistades son muy especial y me gusta tener muchos amistades. Dinero puede comprar muchas cosas en vida que son objectos. Amistades no pueden comprar. Puede hacer muchos amistades en todo el mundo. Amistades traen sonrisas, momentos especiales y mas. Cuando tenía un amistad puede decir todas a su amigo/a. Puede preguntar para su ideas sobre muchas cosas. Dinero no puede hablar. Tengo una amiga que es muy importante ami. Ella es muy sympatico y cuando necesito a ella, ella está allí para mi . Dar gracias para amistades porque cuando todo esta mal, tengo amistades que pueden ayudarme en mi situacion. Hay muchos tipos de amistades; tengo un amistad con mi madre que es muy diferente. Pienso en ella como un ayudante. Siempre dame aconsejos sobre mis problemas. Me encanta a elle mucha. Tengo un amistad con mi hermano. Dice la verdad sobre situaciones a mi todas los tiempos. Amistades pueden ser conmigo siempre en mi vida. Dinero no puede dar todas las cosas que amistades ofrecen. Amistades ofrecen opurtunidades que dinero no puede ofrecen. Me gustan amigos!!!

STAGE V SPANISH

The Value of Friendship

Yo creo que amistad es mas importante que dinero porque amistad es siempere alli pero dinero no es. Cuando yo tengo una problema con dinero ~~mas~~ mis amigos me ayudarán con mi problema. Amistad es mas importante a mi proque mis amigos tienen siempre me ayudan. ~~a~~ Ellos vienen a mi casa cuando ellos saben que yo estoy enferma. Cuando yo tuve mono mi amiga llama Rosita me dio una carta y cuando mi apendix toque out mis amigos me dio globos. Cuando yo lucho con mis padres yo llamo mis amigos porque ellos me hacen estado muy bien. Dinero es no para internidad y amistad sería. Dinero es una cosa que una persona tiene que trabajar para, asi es amistada pero dinero terminará si tu luchas con su superior. En el otro mana amistad posible a curar si una lucha es presente.